Black Baptist

Muslim Mystic:

From the Cosmos

Poems, Lyrics and Journaling

Tasleem Jamila el-Hakim

BLACK BAPTIST MUSLIM MYSTIC:
From the Cosmos

In search of The Most High...

*My
Soul
Speaks*

Copyright© 2013 Tasleem Firdausee

All Rights Reserved. No part of this book may be reproduced in any form by any electronic or mechanical means (including photocopying, recording, or information storage and retrieval) without permission in writing from the author. First Edition 2013
ISBN-978-0-615-92123-5
ISBN-10: 061592123X

To order books or for additional information: www.tasleemjamila.com
773.599.9213

Editor: Debra Ali
Cover Photos (Front & Back): Khalid el-Hakim Cover Design: Kurt Jackson
Interior Layout and Design: Tasleem Jamila el-Hakim
Printed in the United States of America:
My Soul Speaks Publishing
Founded in 2007
www.tasleemjamila.com

MY SOUL SPEAKS PUBLISHING

Thanks and Dedication:

I thank Allah for everything! I thank my beautiful husband Khalid el-Hakim for constant love and inspiration... Mother (Annie), Father (Norman) for endless guidance and support, my beautiful daughters: Maryam, Khalilah for being my pure joy, Bonus Babies: Keisha, BreAna Nieces and Nephews: Jamal, Jabari, Jhordan, Jadyn, Jamila, Autumn Sisters: Norma (twin), Kimberly, Naomi (in memory and spirit) Marlene. Grandma Lena (who is always with me), Grandpa Norman and Grandma Mabel (who are embedded in my soul) Other Mothers: Elaine, Dorothy. To the Turner, Watts, Bell, Kent and Milben family. Sister friends who put up with me and encouraged me whether I ever told them or not: Angela, Areta, Evin, Kelli, Nicole, Stacey, Shierece, Aaliyah, Jacinda, Yavonka (19), Kalimah, Rasheedah, Taheerah, Ndidi, Aya, Kauthar, Carol, Saidah, Sonia, Mariama, Arlene, Ihssan, Shaketa, Jessica, Piper, Invincible, At Peace, Yogi, My brothers: John Jelks, Julian, Robert, Don, Aki, Asad, Thorvelle, D-Nick, Isa, Aaron, FX, Griff, Yahya, Luqman, Amir S, Floyd, Calvin, Carlos, Opio, Jermaine, Reginald, Khari L, Khari B, Tahir, Ishmail, DJSP1, D-Steele, RawPower, Tony S, Dre', Buddy H, Sid, Kevin, Calvin, John, Preach, Nate, Kurtnice, Ismail, Noble MC, Omari, Duminie; The best drummer on the planet who believed in me Fred Puhos Alexander,

Teachers/Ancestors: Honorable Elijah Muhammad, Honorable Marcus Garvey,

Malcolm X, Betty Shabazz, Harriet Tubman, Imam Warith Deen Mohammed, Imam Talib, Sheikh Rashied, Sheikh Nazim, Bro. Kelan Phil Cohran, Honorable Minister Farrakhan, Reverend Johnson,

For All my Chi-town Poets and Emcees who inspired me: Deana Deen, Yahdana, Triple Blak, June June, Phoinex, Zain, Jaqunda, Cap D, Lady Flip, Stepstool, Juice, Momentum

I've been blessed to travel with my poems and my voice lyrically healing from Ghana, West Africa, London, Atlanta, New York, DC and everywhere in between.

Here are a few names of people who looked out for me on the road: Christie Z and Fable, Amal, Latina, Royal, Rasheed, Dr. Saliva, Tahir, Ali, Win.

To all those who prayed for me and cried hearing my poems, I thank you. All those who gave me positive energy in the crowds of festivals, coffee houses, jails, churches, masjids, cafes, schools, sidewalks and anywhere I have performed.

AND THANK YOU!

Why I am writing this book?

First of all, I have thousands of poems that need to be published to the pages for generations to come to have in their library; to sit with literary friends and colleague; to contribute to the world of poets on ink; to let my students know that reading is a gateway to a new world, eternity, imagination, portals of knowledge. The unknown.

I come from parents who read daily any and everything. My mother told me she read every day when I was in the womb with my twin sister. My entire family still is advent readers. My daughters always have books in their hands. I want to stress the importance of the written as well as the spoken word. I've been known for over a decade now for my performance poetry. So welcome to the world of my poetry on page! Not just on stage!

Why did I name it Black Baptist, Muslim Mystic: from the Cosmos?

Let me break it down step by step

Black: Black is the dark matter of space where creativity is formed, the womb of the mother and the mind, Man/Woman is mind, I am a Black woman, I have experiences being Black on this planet and growing up in a Black neighborhood in America. I create and manifest greatness from the dark meditations/visions. Like deep dark moist soil comes nourishment and light.

Black: enveloped in darkness; absorbing light.

Baptist: I grew up going to a Baptist Church as a child. My father is still a deacon and he baptized members as long as I can remember. He is the best man I know, a man of his word. I grew up singing in the choir, going to Sunday school, summer bible camp, being an usher, candy stripe and very involved in Church; dancing in a Gospel dance touring company etc. It has a lot to do with my moral values even today. I still sing old school spiritual songs that are embedded in my soul. These songs came from my ancestors to get us through hard times rejoicing in the Creator. And I still rejoice with them!

Mystic: Someone who lives and delves in truth beyond just this physical realm. In every pulse I see the divine direction.

I've always been in touch with the spirit realm, this came from my grandmother and mother, so it was common to hear and see what is unseen to some growing up. Then as a young adult I was introduced to the Way in Islam some call Sufism, which was so natural to me. So I share poems from that journey that is still a continuation in my journey today. Those who endeavored to create and experience and embody and live a personal relationship with the Divine.

Muslim: I converted to Islam and started calling myself a Muslim in my teen years. It is one who strives to submit her will/life to that of the Creator; Allah. When I became Muslim I wanted to be a minister; a messenger striving to be pious and pleasing to my Lord.

So I know now this is my way of ministering; my poetry; my story; my words.

From the Cosmos?

Cosmos is everything that exists anywhere, studied the evolution of the universe within; inner-verse.

In my path I feel a connectedness to all and everyone striving for knowledge of their divine selves, that essence that we all stem from. Blackness, Nothingness, Baptist, Muslim, Mystic from the Cosmos and beyond.

So I present to you ...

Black Baptist, Muslim Mystic: from the Cosmos

FOREWORD

Welcome to the world of Tasleem Jamila el-Hakim, a Muslim American woman of African descent; a soul manifested here, and now, on a timeless cosmic journey. She is a conscious daughter of the universe, born of a seed planted in African soil, then borne aloft on the winds of time, to the West. She is a country girl born in the city, enveloped by a loving mother's song and nurtured in a home of sewing, art, and creativity, protected by a proud father.

Tasleem Jamila is a Muslim woman word-warrior, a loving daughter to her parents, equally loving mother to her daughters, and adoring wife to her warrior artist husband, Khalid. His photo is on the cover of this book - he of manifest potent images, even as she is a woman of the same. Together they are one; moving infinitely in concentric orbits of spiritual power, in submission to The Lord and Creator of all.

Enter her kingdom, O you seeking inspiration! Bathe in her words and be healed. Bask in her glow and be warmed by the rays emanating from her soul.

Listen and you will hear the ancient Motherland drums of welcome, welcoming, welcome. Read her words and be carried through time and space. Wade in baptismal waters of the sacred griot word, and be touched by The Spirit. Take the long way around avoid random gunfire from self-hating young Black Americans in the inner cities; masters of fratricide men seeking innocent bystander victims. Instead, embrace love and compassion, education and enlightenment, upliftment of self and community, and authentic brotherhood and sisterhood. As you listen with your heart, you will be sustained through the remembrance of (Almighty God) Allah, and protected by His Grace. Partake. You are indeed blessed.

Imam Al-Hajj Talib 'Abdur-Rashid

CONTENTS

I'm Ready	1
The Calling	3
BLACK BAPTIST	**4**
I'm From	5
Sang Gurl	7
My Father, Down South, Down Home	9
Round Table Every Evening at 6pm	11
The Red Line El-Train	13
When Scorpio and Leo Meet	15
Psychic Lady	16
Chuuch	18
Englewood	20
Chi-Town City Life	23
Can't Play Outside Alone	27
Ghetto Queen/Ghetto Princess	29
My Brother, My King	31
Soul Re-birthed	34
Mabel Mae	36
I Write	39
Sold Your Soul?	40
Hard Times (Part 1)	44
Hard Times (Part 2)	46
Never Our Souls	49
Lyrical War	52
City Blues	55
MUSLIM MYSTIC	**57**
I'm Coming	58

Welcome to Reality Check	61
Nation of Islam	64
Excellence Thriving	66
When My Drop Becomes the Ocean	69
Function From the Soul	72
He Live For Justice	75
Assault on the Senses	76
Taking It to the Streets	80
Calm Spirit	83
Divine Love	85
God is One	91
A Brighter Day	94
Tasleem's Bliss	97
Love Transcends Space and Time	98
From the Southside of the Sun	101
Where the love?	102
Motivation	103
Reflection of Beauty	106
Journal Entry- NYC	108
Back em' Them Days	109
What If	113
We Never Ran	116
League of Assassins	118
Eternal Soul	119
Came for Solace	121
I Am Who I Say I Am	124
Naqshbandi Way	126
FROM THE COSMOS	**128**
Ever Flowing	129
Music is Life	130
Bro Kelan Phil Cohran	132

Dedicate	134
The Saints Come Out at Night	135
Warriors Cry! Warrior's Cry!	137
Seven	139
Leaders of a New School	140
I Am	141
Belle Isle Awakening	143
Malnutrition (Drive to Be Alive)	144
We Still Screaming for Freedom	149
One With the One	154
Real Power	156
Yearning	157
Healing Our Wounds	159
Pure Soul	161
90's on the Scene	163
Peace and Reason	165
Hold On	166
Love Catch Me	167
Balance	168
Me	169
Infinite Elevations	171
Letter to My Grandma	174
4AM- The Opening	175
Rising	180
They Sent Me	182
Tasleem Jamila el-Hakim-Bio	185

I'm Ready

When I write, I want my words to be so
authentic every syllable and rhyme to get in
it
inside beats to exhale between each
sentence so you inhale my soul and feel
Centered.

I find wisdom in the most unfamiliar places
Spaced on sidewalks and street corners
adjacent
not always in classrooms and boardrooms
but in God's hidden faces
like Ray-Ray and Pookie, Shaquitta and
shorties with loose laces.

Reaching mastery through struggles with
detour and blocked roads
Sometimes can't see clear got stopped
cold yellow tape, red zones
Strength in experience so I never
let go just explode
with new vision
God permission and uploading ancient
superior codes and wisdoms.

When faced with pain it triggered unstoppable
forces within me, to mend me, turn and spin
me, into my original essence; the twin me.

So I ask God to send me to battle cause I'm
ready for war, ready for war.

I'm possessed with the best yes I'm blessed on all sides.

So send me to battle cause I'm ready for war, ready for war.
Representing the God-dome so freedom is naturally mine.

THE CALLING

These poems will save
These poems you crave

You've prayed
I've slayed
Midnight muses manifest on page
Unlock the cage
Ignite the sage
Spiritual warrior rage

These are literary coding
Ancient cosmic folding

This is a transcription of my mind and heart

This is an unpacking
A breaking through and cracking
A full expansion, no lacking

Black Baptist

"Your voice is soothing to the soul, so don't be afraid to get it out and Sang Girl!"
Mama Coleman

I'm from

I'm from a place where innocence is kept
Elders wept for souls of those who slept

Who crept from moral excellence and steered left

Yet hope hopped all around 95th street,
where brief moments of wisdom
leaped

All mothers on the block were my mom
calm, candid and wise like psalms

On Sunday on my way to church, first memories of preaching, Christian teachings, reaching from down south roots.

Rev. Johnson hummed in a perfect pentatonic African tone

I ushered down aisles with white gloves symbolic of purity and divine love

I'm from where mom cooked everything from scratch

No boxes, cans, frozen or prepared poisons camouflaged as nutrition

with psychic mamas' intuition who knew how to guide

I reminisce; remember those endless days
Grandma's words ageless; she is the ultimate sage

Constantly prays from that African Native way
so I glided into growing and knowing real
womanhood
Womanhood with divine purpose

No worthless breaths were breathed from Dad
he had, gentle quiet fierce silence that turned
all good from bad

He knew how to summon up the spirits to
mend any situation

And well, with this; gumbo mosaic of childhood
reality
molded me, created who I be

Deep moist roots with fertile soil, that didn't
fall far from the tree.

SANG GURL

Every Sunday I sang in the sunshine
band and I felt like Sunshine when I sang

I knew it was my calling; my healing my souls
connecting to pure bliss.

I had the lead vocals because I was bold
Singing about my Lord and Jesus made me feel
whole

As the congregation clapped

my Dad the head Deacon tapped feet
to the piano and organ Standing
next to Norma and Morgan it
brought a pure sparkle

My heart was wrapped with the security of the
gospel

some got the holy ghost I
was warm as fresh toast

Jesus loves me and Amazing Grace were my
favorite hymns

The chords worked my lungs like going to the
gym

My big sister Kim looked in the front pew with
a proud grin

I was told to be loud as if they could hear us in
the heavens
On the next planet.

*"Jesus love me,
this I know, for the Bible tells me so"*

Praising God gives me spiritual
glow Room to grow

Expanded heart so young and innocent
voice is the original instrument,
praising is my natural stimulant

*Jesus loves me this I know for the Bible tells
me so.*

My Father, Down South, Down Home

Pack up the Ford pickup truck
Mechanically perfect with oil,
gas and new tires

So we won't get stuck
on the road to roots
Memories planted
blessings granted
love enchanted
Mama chanted
kinfolk transplanted.

Summer routine, from a baby to my teens in between Chicago and Mississippi grounds
Daddy, uncles, aunts and cousins would be found
on the road to the red sand
Grand Daddy's land
That he preserved for us from my great, great grand parents
who believed in owning and claiming your own
Bordering and keeping a safe zone, so generations today still call it home

Rivers and streams and outhouses and night star gleams
We rode horses with long ponytails
fished in rivers catching whiting, catfish and snails
Whatever Grandpa hunted,

Grandma gravy up and we ate without complaint or frown
With gratefulness and reverence, cause then we had manners
Now that mattered.

Along the way we had cousins in every state cause we believed in procreating and being fruitful
We multiplied; yes to God we were dutiful
100's of cousins, how beautiful

Burying feet in red sand for healing
tuned in on my heritage
where slaves once meditated on
freedom, And I hear the messages in the sand

Red, Rich, soul where my Daddy was born
so I don't feel torn, between city and country

They blend together like a perfect DJ Ron Hardy House music mix
Like Rakim's rhymes tongue smooth and swift like cold Chicago winds that kick

I am naturally nurtured by both.

Round Table Every Evening at 6pm

Round table discussion at 6pm in the Turner household
Behold, revelation, knowledge, healing and wisdom to behold

Peas, cornbread, steak, mashed potatoes, green beans and okra
Back then no TV distractions with Oprah

The school
where
families
prayed
talked of
their day
so children
wouldn't sway
and be left to
streets for prey

Where simple sounds of chewing were rhythmic and poetic

Where speech was clean with no outdoor remnants or rhetoric

Where Kool-Aid was red, purple and sometimes even green

And Daddy's serious looks were sometimes mistaken as mean,

Where best behavior was practiced
and learned parents' stories taught
that you get what you earn

Teaching us how to deal with differences in the world with respect
and the Lords' prayer so our soul we'd never neglect

Dinner time so precious and historical
wisdom implanted was sometimes simple and sometimes metaphorical
sometimes literal and sometimes allegorical.

This is the experience that I wonder if more had it; would bond hearts

Would wash out disrespectful children and families wouldn't be like broken parts

Dinnertime, a time for
joy in eating, assigned
seating,

Family hellos and daily check in
and greetings every voice was
heard no competing

Sacredness of every opinion
was revered with parents'
guidance of course to steer in
the direction of purpose and
the divine in order to blossom

into what I am still becoming today.

The Red Line- EL-Train (Chicago)

The el train mainly the RED line was an adventure every day
Like I was Dorothy in the Wiz and Alice in wonder of my land

It was like an eastern market where you could purchase even your groceries
Vertical blinds, barrettes, candy, oil, incense, jackets, bus cards, food stamps, credit cards, batteries

And like B-king have it your way
if they didn't have it yesterday, they had it today and what tomorrow would bring I couldn't wait till the next day

Chains getting snatched quick like a magic trick
Money swindles from card games played slick

Puffed up pride like fluffy cheetos
Chicago thugs had big egos

Better be careful what hood you entered, wrong color from the rainbow might be released back like a placenta

And the b-boys rhyming for a penny or dollar Chi-town south side flow like Common

or Westside flava quick like Twista
Telling stories of shoot outs and fine sisters

This train speed from 95th street to Howard up North
It was obvious where the color line divided, downtown faces got lighter and trains got crowded

Language became bilingual and diverse
but no matter what you still had to watch your purse

B-boys still flipped and emcees got down

on the way to the Sub-T on the north side of town
You saw smiles, blank faces and frowns

But it was always an adventure on the EL
I could write an entire series on all the unique stories to share.

When Scorpio and Leo Meet
(for my Scorpio Mommy)

FIRE!!! FIRE!!! FIRE!!!

Flames blasting from our actions
burning up all negative forces within reach
HOT ORANGE SUN RULED SPIRIT
take over whatever she pursues

FIRE!!! FIRE!!! FIRE!!!

It purifies to awaken to anew
it cleanses all dirt and debris in
view Reflecting light from the
cosmos,
cause most of our dreams are bright in reality

FIRE!!! FIRE!!! FIRE!!!

When the CREATOR created this union
The Most High was smiling with sunshine
cycles
born on the cycles of the sun
giving, giving, giving light in all we do

FIRE!!! FIRE!!! FIRE!!!

Step to us with truth and reality… and
we will light a match and cure you of
any ails
cause when Scorpio and LEO meet,
LOVE prevails.

Psychic Lady

(for my Mommy and Grandmommy)

I saw wisdom on her forehead and eternity in her face

Predicted like Nostradamus future activities that'll take place

We placed her on high with the psychics and sometimes said she's a lil' psycho

not yet comprehending intuition, telepathy and soul; spirit marriage

She brushed us off so eloquently as she foretold our events

knowing her seeds better then they knew themselves

She'd lived in realms and dimensions beyond our imagination at the time

Numerology, psychology, Herb logy she studied it all, nothing was out of bounds or line

Long thick jet black hair was her royal pride curvy figure with a southern stride

Loved her people with a soulful passion talked of freedom, justice and healing daily

Remembered the Ku Klux Klan terrorizing her childhood

Remembered Alabama's segregation and African memory of degradation

so she always claims and reps Chicago where memories are more free
where Blues met her at the border
She is strength and power all rolled in a 5'3 frame
can read you inside out before you speak
serious about you practicing what you preach
She'd say, "don't just say it do it, talk is cheap"
Told me you're human you can do what anyone can do the same or better,
Tap your source and your natural clever
be yourself you're infinite, boundless and forever
So tangled in that old time religion which is our natural self
she knew nothing else
Gave me love of blues, BB King and Bobby Blue Bland
Sharpened my pencils when I walked to school to take a stand
Told me, yes, Deb, yes you can!

Birthed 5 eternities in the modern world
five gorgeous little girls

Perfect nurturer at home and in the streets
unique, so I learned to walk to my hearts beats
Unraveled the mystery of herself and shared
comforted us when we were confused, battered and scared

Still watching - *Psychic Lady*
Over her big grown baby!!!

CHUUCH

Ruffled dress, ruffled socks and patent leather shoes
Peppermints in pocket, bible in purse and in my right hand Sunday dues
called a truce on Saturday night and turned off the down home blues
Gospels and spirituals filled the
rooms it's time for Sunday School!

Early mornings, homemade biscuits, grits, eggs and cheese
Mamas cooking was fresh to deaf cause she aimed to please
The palates perfectly prepped for dinners' meat, potatoes and peas.

Jumped in the American Made automobile
cause my uncles worked in Detroit at GM
as if one purchase would secure their jobs
but we never had Hondas, Toyotas or Saabs

Straight to church no stops in between entering
the chapel where conduct was serene happy to
greet my cousins, Jennifer and Christine

Angelic spirits embraced the
atmosphere Sunday classes were here
Praise the Lord was the regular cheer
it put me in gear for moral discipline in life

foundational roots with good intentions were right

Memorized verses, choir rehearses
hymns were hummed to keep away the curses

Spirituals made some so high they'd holy ghost in the pew
My aunt screamed every week, saying she had to let the energy come through
I'd wait to pass her until she was through
it would astonish me every time as if it was new
The ushers came with handkerchiefs and fans they knew just what to do

Church was filled with families and generational members
weekly congregation from Januarys to Decembers
A spiritual family who really cared
hurt, joy, healing, pain and prayers we shared,

You can go away physically but experience no one can kill
peel away the decades and my early beginnings are revealed
Every layer lifts me to add to my journeys
thrills armed with strong armor my aura has shields This is heart stamped and sealed.

ENGLEWOOD

In the slums spirits are numb and they easily succumb to the mindset of bums

but when you think they are done when you think there are none

a few warriors have come, a few warriors have come, a few warriors have come

They used to walk to the beat of the drums
They used to walk to the beat of the drums

As I walk through the slums
Where spirits are numb
Where they die when they're young

Where some don't even get out of the bed till the setting of the sun
or the setting of a mother's son
Who America has shunned

Who still question, has freedom really rung?
Who are mostly the indigenous people of the earth who walked to the beat of the drums.

When they were born into this world I swear their eyes were so wide and vibrant they could see past the moon

Now they're mentally, physically and spiritually out of tune

They got a neighborhood triangle from home,
store front church to corner store

Where they give you salaams, sell you salami,
liquor and a pack of Moores

but their souls are searching for so much more
14 years of age Brianna and Marquietta
they thirst for more

But they're afraid to reflect on their
reflection so they just avoid looking in the
mirror

They're afraid of seeing their true reality
approaching nearer

They got yellow tape and white chalk bodies
that line the street

While they walk around all day licking on their
fingers from those hot chips that they eat

for breakfast, lunch and dinner,
and in between they talk about

"Imma be a superstar

*and I gotta gets me a man with them tight
rims on his car"*,

This is the hood

Where their lips are wrapped around
blunts and weed,

Cristal and greed

the neighborhoods in need

Their souls are so frozen they forget to
breathe living that dysfunctional way
so many dysfunctional days

I wish that they knew that they were spirited
being

sent here on earth to contribute with spirited seeing,

I wish that they knew that from generation to generation that positive energy could link
And they don't have to give in to what their homies think

And Allah can change things in a
blink but I just see their spirits shrink,

They're emotionally tangled systematically mangled,

But I pray that Allah may have used me if even to influence one

and that's what motivates me

So I don't fear; fear tactics that try and harass me

Even if they threaten to blast me,

I know with Allah they won't get past me,

and I know that they won't out last me
because...

I discovered a few reincarnated warrior
bones resurfacing in the hood
in a place tucked away in Chi-town

called ***Englewood***

Intro to Chi-City Life

More than a dime piece
lyrics make your mind freeze

I'm a Leo linking linguistic lost legacies and
quoting around the commas and parenthesis

My rhymes be supersonic,
melodic like its Quranic
Coming straight from the
Chi
the south side is where I reside...

CHI-TOWN CITY LIFE

They used to get down real, real gritty
life in the city

Was not always pretty
some even called me sadity,
like I was from the suburbs
Where they called blunts, herbs,

Where some faked happiness but they really emotionally disturbed,

Where there are no sidewalks and curbs.

Chi town Southside is where I'll have a happy childhood and in my teen years,
experience some tricky living

Grew up with close family and friends

and then got introduced to some back stabbers with sticky fibbing

Little girls fell face flat in the fantasies the big city painted that caused them to see things you'd say were unforgiving

My parents had KKK memories from Alabama and Mississippi living

They migrated to Chi-town for a better life
Chi-town would bring them some happiness, some strength, some stress, some strain and some strife

I hung out in the hood in Princeton Park and the Lowden Homes and rode in 9-8 rides

and if you came around my way with the wrong color on, you better hide

because GD's and Blackstone's didn't coincide
the streets were filled with liquor bottles and old dirty condoms
but we still had some Black pride

I had to erase, escape and exchange the negative mindset that permeated from 95th street to the wild 100's,

from Princeton Park to Jackson Blvd

times were good but for some times were hard
Even Chicago Public Schools taught me
nothing but how to dodge bullets and how to cut class,
and how to do just enough to get by and just enough to pass

Pre-natal abortions and synthetic misuse
neglected souls that always had an excuse
But my Mom, she always talked about revelation

and my soul reeked of revolution

and my Daddy was a physical example of that inner city evolution

Ridding our family of those inner city pollutions

So when chaos reigned in the streets

my household was like a spiritual retreat
nourished with scriptures to eat

They first taught me I had my own demons to defeat

that's when I realized my spirit and my mind had to meet

My soul was crying to be
free it was dying to be free
but sometimes I didn't hear the divine in me

My spirit was staticky and sometimes I couldn't hear it

Disconnected from my soul and disconnected from my spirit

It took much pain and introspection to free my spirit

And that's why I sharpen my tongue

for those crack addicted brothers and sisters, my abused aunts and my mom
never tiring of my mission

Now my soul finally fell in total submission

and now it's cooler on the east side of chi-town where the sun shines

Allah allowed my words to be a healing that vibrates throughout the universe even past chi-town

And now I meditate, contemplate and prostrate east

Found my way of life my contentment my peace; Al-Islam,

Now my inner being is blessed and it's bursting like bombs

And now I meditate on the psalms and the Quran

and I see my spiritual lifeline in my palms.

What's life in the Chi
A struggle just to get by
Seems like I'm chasing the sky
What's life in the Chi
What's life in the Chi

CAN'T PLAY OUTSIDE ALONE

The Jim Crow era where KKK openly lynched for amusement

Ropes from trees so the visual could torture the souls of Black people

White dolls for beautiful brown babies to play with

with no replicas of their beauty

Separate water fountains and entrances to restaurants and shops

so they wouldn't remember their royalty entering in the front

Had to call white children their same age Mr. or Miss

Having to see their people slave so hard for so little

Stories of the KKK riding past their childhood home with burning crosses and anger and devilish hate in their eyes

Scaring little brown babies and Fathers, uncles and anyone in view

Memories followed them from Mississippi and Alabama to Illinois and Michigan too,

So they never could play outside alone

Escape to the north and we will have freedom they said, escape to the north and we will have freedom they said?

Well 60 years later in the streets of Chicago
blood is running down drains on walkways,
Streets stay lined in white chalk,

Replacing hop scotch with colorful chalk
thugs with no love at home creep and
stalk

negative profiling and on the corner decadent
talk

Mother won't take a walk around the block
because she's afraid to be shot

attacked by Brown because she is brown and
elderly

But still no desire to move back to the southern
states

Her heart is in Chicago, high school proms,
babies born, wedding bliss

So she finds freedom in books and meditation
and telephone conversations and pictures of
grandbabies and biscuits

She stares out the window reminiscing on the
old days

Waiting for one of her grown daughters or sons
for safety to come and sit with her on the patio

And after all these years
She still,

Can't play outside alone.

Ghetto Queen/Ghetto Priestess
(Lyrics to a song dedicated to my students @ Dunbar High School)

She was only 16
She let any man lie between
She had no self-esteem
She thought she knew everything
But I still could hear, I still could hear I
still could hear her soul sing

Growing up in the ghetto

Ideal of beauty was hot pants and stilettos
Never dove inside

Or stimulated her 3rd eye.
More than bird's fly

She didn't know she could spiritually fly
She was too busy getting an artificial high

Kissed her soul goodbye

She was only 16
She let any man lie between
She had no self-esteem
She thought she knew everything
But I still could hear
I still could hear
I still could hear her soul sing

One day she ran into her spiritual friend
Twisted fate she became her best friend.
Years of pain turned into victory to ascend

She was forced to search within

Internalized her years of sin for healing
Because she numbed her soul from feeling

Now she beams a light
Found her spirit so bright
Her whole being is faced to the right

She was only 16
She used to let any man lie between
Now she has self-esteem
She thought she knew everything

Deep dark piercing eyes like the Massai, Anpu sight so see wise

Activated her inner cosmic zone
Sat on her queen throne

And I still can hear
I still can hear
I still can hear her soul sing

I knew it was coming I
knew it was coming

Because I could always hear her soul sing I could always hear her soul sing.

My Brother, My King

Hustle and scuffle just to get it
in so my soul won't sit in sin
Grinding, grinding got to make them
ends
real men taking care of his kin

He said,
I'm working 60 hours a week
jerking cause man 168 hours with no sleep
body tweaks, hustling on feet, this getting deep
Not a dad that's deadbeat
making bread,
that's concrete because
streets don't sleep
Man she bittersweet
Shady ones' cheat, I'm upright on beat
game tight on feet, same fight like Master P
Independent grinding, but you constantly
finding and purposely maligning my character
Feel like a convict on the run
just to get a sneak peak of my son
Chill Hun
I wanna know
him to grow him
play baseball and show him
Single mom that's a beast waiting to throw him
A crease waiting to fold him
A feast waiting to swallow hold
him

Like yeast I want to mold him
That's my seed I gotta sow him
plant knowledge and wisdom so the streets won't grow him

He worked hard to the bone
Ran yards to get home
Taking care of his own
taught me to stare in that zone
taught me what's fare cause he's grown
Bills paid gas, electric and phone
Kept us fi with coach glasses, eclectic and Gucci cologne
and to stay away from them boys on the corner
Gave us security at home
raised me with surety, I'd never roam
A father you wish you could clone
A father king on the throne, with that Mississippi mentality, no excuses just top morality, southern hospitality, that Jesus personality, cause it's a miracle he kept us from the vicious streets of the Chi some called reality.

Treats my mom like a supreme queen
Life like a Cosby show scene
Gave me an example of real family love as a teen
It was so right like fun things
So light like sun beams

Taught me about them boys as a teen
Spirit hot like sunbeams
so bright I need sunscreen

So bright my soul sings
Like Mike when he reigned supreme
That's my Dad, my king.

Hustle and scuffle just to get it in

So my soul won't sit in sin, grinding, grinding, got make them ends

Real men taking care of his kin
Real men taking care of their kin
Real men taking care of their kin

And some Dads are single
at home Saturday night can't mingle

A smile from his baby's face makes his soul tingle

Real men sacrificing from the soul,
Conditions didn't numb the soul,
In the neighborhood on patrol.

Soul Re-birthed

America just left this little black girl withered
her soul torn and quivered
Nations rise from her womb
Every man's playground but her doom
Pale skinned complex
told brown and black was a hex
Thickness of her forehead and
lips
was only victim to massa getting between them hips.

Self-worth
battered
Self-love shattered
Self-hate carried on through her tears to her babies
Never revered as a real lady.

But through it all this Godly woman did rise
All her glory is now being uncovered from society's disguise
Her connection onto her Lord is
clear
Love for herself one God she fears
Knows her origin is from her divine mother Eve
Draws that energy from her heart to conceive
Spiritual warriors building nations
whether she is from Africa, America, Asian, Haitian,
turning herself east

meditating on her God within
Activating her divine attributes like the prophets who are her kin
With God she's properly aligned
no longer spiritually blind

Every woman must be aligned spiritually and connected
Uproot your passions be on high and respected,

And those who knew not their worth, will experience *'a glorious rebirth.*

Mabel Mae
(For my Grandma's, Mabel and Lena Mae)

We got mental and spiritual trauma that hasn't been dealt.

Numb on false fictional pleasures and haven't really felt

our detrimental state of mind that still carries on today.

Massa just said, *"you free"* and now we think we okay?

We had no parental, environmental or mental training and it still shows cause now we sway from our spiritual roots that is embedded in our genes.

Our bloodline stems from Kings and Queens reigned on thrones for centuries before our captivity.

We were on the siratul mustaqeen, royalty, dynamic and serene.

Worshipped Allah in a state of peace and divine realty

Spiritual from all nations living according to Divine Laws; we knew how to be

role models for generations to be spiritual warriors that could carry onto eternity.

Never nodded or slept on our duty to our Lord. Never neglecting our soul that was our reality before the ships we were to board.

(Great great great great Grandma Mable Mae)

Im' Mable Mae an I jus wans to
say even tho iz physicallis enslaves
I knew Allah sets the reals way.

He shows me visions in mys dreams
that we's were mo than this.

Not living in slop shacks , hog eatin and smellin like piss.

I knows I might not in this life be's physicallys free
but I's gots faith that my offsprings gones be
on the righteous paths theys stoles from me.

My faith n' Islams runs through my veins

and it's gone resurface and one day we's gone reign.

(Tasleem Jamila)

Yeah that was my great, great, great grandma Mable Mae.

I'm one of the *ones* she saw in that vision that day.

Even though I come from psychological and mental abuse,

born and raised in the inner city ghetto as a youth

Allah raised one up cause it's time for Mable Mae's dreams to come into existence

For me to come back to Islam and be persistent.
Weaved in my soul is the Arabic letters and vibrations.
Stamped on my heart is the Quran and written revelations,
and engraved in my being is the dhikr; the lost chants of my ancestors.
Laillahailallah, there is no God but God.
And tattooed on my soul is Quran and recitations.

I am so blessed to be one of the chosen
If you deeply contemplate on this and the time we're in...

It should leave you frozen.

I Write
(Journaling/Free write with my students at Dunbar High School)

I write to nourish my soul within

Ascending from the depths of faults not perfect but striving for that perfection

of self

Through words

I write to speak for the countless ancestors' whose voices were left on pause,

halted, stopped forced to speak through the hums or drums

I write to increase love

Love for the possibilities and everything that surrounds it

I am a vessel open to be used for the divine

I write for the children of the cities who are unnamed

Not knowing their original names of the Divine who still don't see their true beauty

I write to lessen the inner pain that I've suffered hoping to heal another soul after reading my words on paper

or hearing my screams in a performance or seeing the reality in my eyes...

I write, I write, I write.

Sold Your Soul?
(Hip-Hop Lyrics)

To thyself be true you got so much so much trapped inside of you
Don't let it hide in you
Rid the greed and false pride in you

Self-sold for talent
Unbalanced, and creatively unchallenged
Sold your soul for your talent
Living life without balance

U got to get paid
just to get 5 minutes on the stage
Souls locked in a cage
to get a write up in the Source full page

Youth looking at you in aw
Mouth hanging open from the jaw
Label sucking your spirit with a straw
Hearts grown cold you need to thaw
Blinded 3rd eye, I thought you saw

Corporate giant's pockets get paid
you like a virgin that just got laid.

A generation's lost!
Role models? Doing anything at any cost

Held bondage to this artificial industry
just like they lynched us from a tree
Words from your lips are like debris
Spiritually blind and you can't see
Degrading your mother but you can't
see we made in the image of Thee.

(Chorus)
To thyself be true you got so much, so much
trapped inside of you,
Don't let it hide in you,
Rid the greed and false pride in you.

Your Art and Culture they
exploit
but you exceptionally adroit
Cause we come from the anoint

Everyone but our hood benefits
some see and some just don't
get

Searching for a false
position
they come like a magician
We need a spiritual physician,
God's submission
and old traditions

Ancestors stressed from the negative
press

Our perceptions are sunless,
transgressed and distressed

In need of liberation and
salvation seeds
earning college degrees
come out still weak in your
knees; in need,
Brains in a mental freeze.

Your spirit suffers anxiety
trying to fit into the corrupt society
There are those with God as a
priority the often unseen majority
led to believe the minority.

to uphold this wandering nation
These lost generations

They void of truth
while the masses turning it up and raising the
roof.

Illusions sold to us
Get caught up in the
system
Know thyself and just listen.

Hidden souls will soon come to
light
coming with the One in sight

Real artists are called *underground*?
Not, we over-stand and are over
bound

But what went before must come
around,
evil days are numbered so I expound

For those searching for true self to be found
For those searching for true self to be found
For those searching for true self to be found

(Chorus)
To thyself be true you got so much, so much
trapped inside of you,
Don't let it hide in you,
Rid the greed and false pride in you.

Hard Times (Part 1)

We got hard times
that's why I'm doing hard rhymes
They on the block they doing hard crimes

Days are dark and
we need a spark
and
stop the rhetoric, cheezin and the
talking
Bush still be spying, greezin and stalking

Some don't even know we at war so how can
they fight best
Willie lynched us and we like a corpse laying to
rest
I'm on a warriors' quest
look how they got us all stressed
from the east coast, the west coast and the
Midwest.

I'm here to speak like a rebel
Save souls and crush devils
We need freed souls
the truth got to be told
We ain't free yet
in the ghettos in debt
Mentally deleted, depleted and they souls can
be sold

It hurts to see my peeps in this condition

So I'm on a mission
Allah is gathering those who sick of this edition
My soul is in submission. I ain't no fake musician.

Need more than pickets signs and protest,
I became fearless
so don't be earless

She got hard times
so I speak hard rhymes
while America doing some hard crimes.

They say Palestine is theirs
Darfur catching scares
in need of real powers and prayers

We got short term memory forgetting our history
We steeped in misery

I can't sit here singing kuumbiyah
while the years are passing by
waiting for a god from the sky

I'm trying to keep my spirits up but it's hard when they struggling

Satan smuggling energy so I generate from Allah
So I am used to reactivate near and far.

Hard Times (Part 2)

We got hard times
that's why I'm doing hard rhymes
They on the block they doing hard crimes

While Tim pop locked on the block
Michael cocked glocks and dodged shots from cops
I'm sure Tim was not shocked when Michael got popped
Just a day in the hood some called Hard times and hard knocks

This vicious violent cycle
Hard times for Shaquitta and Michael
Spiritual and physical battle
in the streets brothas rattle
They wanna clone us like cattle
Some have grown cold
while some of us grow bold
Connecting the young and old
Prophesied in the beginning, it's manifesting til the end
When did the hard times begin, man we wasted in sin

We got hard times
that's why I'm doing hard rhymes

They on the block they doing hard crimes

Some say I speak like a rebel,
Save souls and crush devils,
Gas 5 dollars they wanna free you
You gotta free you, but learn to be you

Look what they do, devils trying to chain you and freeze your brain too
Look in the scriptures for clues

Block filled with drugs
American made thugs
with ol' E in mugs

and in between we still got our Quran and prayer rugs

while they infiltrating in our mosques with government bugs

They live deprived
just battling to stay alive

Hood got debris and depression
desperation and oppression
Suppressing thoughts of suicide
they're pushed aside
systemized genocide

Fornicating with their lives
adulterating lies
Dark half lit skies

Filled with denial
even sell their baby for survival
to get the bills paid

my sistas get laid

1000's die young,
Millions cry young Mother's single
raising suns gazing at their sons

Off to try to find manhood on the block with
their cock
or their glock
While their mother's heart stops
ancestors' graves rot

Memories of warriors seem far
but Allah got soldiers that gleam stars...

Never Our Souls

They scattered and battered our minds and bodies and shattered our spirits but never our souls, never our souls, never our souls

We were royalty on the red, black and green continent
Representing the blood, the people and the land and we paid no rent
We were never bent by some false lies some Europeans sent
Until greed and envy took over and the slaves first went, to the western shores and in the Atlantic there are still some of my kin
They were chanting 99 Holy names on the ships in roots Kunte Kente gave hint
of lost spiritual roads to come live at a new residence
where it was sinful to read and speak our own tongue so the elders were lynched
Then we had bastard children with no mothers raised by the deceitful hands,
some of yall don't understand, some of yall don't' understand
Oral stories lost from slave sells of the African man
the old divide and conquer plan
they pimped and raped our
land

We got *some* still afraid to explore, they

continue to ignore
mystical spiritual
paths
Because they afraid of massas wrath

who taught we weren't whole but less than half
They didn't teach use about our souls they just lived by their nafs
Ripped us of our dignity, our humanity and our native crafts

Sometimes at night my fingers still bleed
from genetic cotton picking tendencies
And I know we reap what we sow from our planted seeds
and I know now we can soar at our souls speed

The schemes are publicized, they don't even disguise the lies
and we'll finally realize
that God raises from the ghetto too
and our souls won't be compromised
And then we'll strive for divine presence again like the wise
even though some still pray for our demise

The west shall be the center of piece not the Middle East
We'll rise like yeast
rise like yeast from America the
beast
Then our souls shall feast

Those once beat down shall speak

because the enemies getting real weak
and like hell they gone feel the heat

And like honey it's gonna be so
sweet because self-discoveries at its
peak

We'll hear the indigenous drums coming down
the street

They won't be able to
compete They won't be able
to compete

because God is on our side and well the books
are not all complete!

They scattered and battered our minds and bodies and shattered our spirits but never our souls, never our souls, never our souls

Now the story unfolds

Lyrical War

War of Words
Words! Words! Words!
We been fighting for years with words for reparations/emancipations
every since integration
declined in entrepreneur liberation

Training and tasking in the war
You got to know what you fighting for
Coming with tremendous energy and stamina to avenge and take justice
For the battery and assault of
words the attacks
screams
with deliberate intention
Voices almost mystifying with force
manifest from the spirituals we
sung up sprung a warriors' tongue

We walk in unison from chaos and disorder
in order to heal our souls from the bruises
with war torn excuses
Footpaths imprinted on blood stained
soil
Voices layered over drumbeats roaring
Spirits soaring
Hearts pouring
with freedom and justice like packing
grenades with words of rage

Hiding inside of ghetto boys and girls
tongues blazing with fire

Cause they molested and fondled our freedom
inside our souls' warriors warded off demons
with the words at war

We got lyrical war
tactics
verbal war increased

Representing lyrical war and spiritual
peace Reincarnated ancestors never
deceased
Speaking with authority
Lyrical war lyrically packed with words

*We at war we gotta know what we fighting
for who's keeping score, we gotta know what
we fighting for, it's a spiritual war, we gotta
know what we fighting for, it's a lyrical war,
we gotta know what we fighting for.*

With words we've overcome death
overcome restlessness
Masters of self
visionaries with every
breath
Art of words
lyrical war opening doors
coated with healing
Branded boldness and brave hearts

Piercing darkness through light our words were loud and fierce like the African Drum
Impregnating minds and souls like we waiting on a Savior to come

Lyrically loaded with lots to say
so I'm spiritually swollen so I gots' to pray
Saturated, seeped and soaked with subliminal signs
so words came from holy books sent from the divine

So we're running toward freedom in our voices
Delivering us from slave plantations
Now linking with Abiodun of the Last Poets,
Words that carry the healing vibrations
Through the slave fields, Harlem, and Chicago
yearning liberation

City Blues

This city Blues is inner

Sometimes the stress rush to my head and make my blood thinner

It's like in the hood they eat devastation for dinner

We can't let ol massa be the winner.

In the inner city it's
grimy and gritty
and deceptive political committees

Unfair economic conditions
So I'm on a mission
like a third world country
physician
to transform my peoples condition
back to those ancient traditions
Gotta a new rendition

Slavery was terrorism
and we still
terrorized

But our hood is disguised
with Starbucks and
underlies
so like an archeologist I dig up the
lies where truth resides
where self-hate divides
to be a roadmap and guide.

Expose evil and give hope
then give them ways and means to cope
and some gone be smoked
I still feel the pain on neck from them ropes

There is always a deeper spiritual reality
To save us from this brutality
this sick mentality
with our multiple personalities

It's only an appointed time for this deviltry, evil and corruption
There is an underground revolutionary interruption
boiling up like a volcanic eruption

Because there are soldiers that God is sending
that God is ascending and defending
with no fakeness and pretending
with His unlimited power and force
to divorce us from this demonic course.

Reverse the news
Most been abused
so I'll paint a picture
with my lyrical
scriptures to hit yah
right between your *third eye and heart center.*

MUSLIM MYSTIC

*"The spiritual realm carries it all,
remember that."*
Sheikh Azeem

I'm Coming

I'm coming like a bat out of hell cause' I'm just plain tired
of all the haters on the outside and inside me, they just got fired
My soul is not for hire
My real intentions be God's desires
That's why I'm constantly, continuously and endlessly inspired

Some peoples' negative energy be so thick I can see it before I turn around in the back of me
Coming from the right the left all angles like it's smacking me
trying to figure out where I'm going and what I'm doing
like Malcolm they be tracking me
But God surrounds me like a 100 foot cemented wall against those attacking me
so ain't no back tracking me
On my road to heaven I got to run through hell but I'm leaving poetry pages for generations to decode my warrior trails
It's like I got reincarnated Muhammad and Malcolm X atoms and cells
They say being a little black girl in America you stripped and molested before birth
so as a baby my first thirst was to be quenched with knowledge and wisdom when I was nursed

So I wouldn't just stay hyped up never devoting just quoting the latest Quran or Bible verse

I'm the daughter of those martyred, slaughtered, saints and headstrong

Who worked in 100-degree weather and carried babies on their hips and their back bones

Who knew they were spiritual first and led victory at war, they made salat at Martyrs tombstones

In any adversity they kept strong

In the city and suburbs everybody's confused

Illusional lifestyles misused

So called role models?

Even their parents confused

They need to eat my words for breakfast so they'll have some real nourishment before school

Bathe and baptize in my lyrics so in the summertime they'll stay cool

Most people are phony they're transparent they're see through

It's kind of like we all cross-eyed because when we look at each other we see two

Because some just can't see truth

They're backed up like 50 years of backed up semen

Fake flossing on the outside but inside there screaming

because they're too impatient to reach their own demons

God is taking me through struggle to end at my perfection
to completely cure and heal any of my imperfections
I'm going to be like those who are no longer in need of reading books to teach
I'm gonna be like those who believe in God's power to reach
I'm gonna be like those whose actions line up with the words that they speak

Yall it's real out here
People stay stressed, depressed hyped up and they stay blunted
That's why I don't stay stagnated and stunted
And I'm striving hard and well I'm restless but never breathless

That's why I gotta come like a bat outta hell because I'm just plain tired
of all the haters on the outside and inside, but they just got fired
My soul is not for hire
My real intentions be God's desire
that's why I'm constantly, continuously and endlessly inspired

I'm a revolutionary freeing souls'
without retire.

Welcome to Reality Check

It was a long day, seemed like the longest by far
I decided to walk and not drive in the car
Feeling *floaty*, fearless and fierce
Beautiful blue dress, yes I was surely blessed.

I had good intentions
thought I'd mention
It was the first day I covered my hair with a scarf
Mind was in the stars
Felt like a Queen
Self-love on high vibrating self-esteem
People on the block looked at me with a new respect
My way of life; Islam was feeling correct
Smiles of peace were sent my way
Oh Allah! What a glorious day!

Went into the corner store side door to enter
Salaams came from behind the counter
but I still had to encounter,
a dirty, filthy store in my
hood I never understood
why they didn't live around us and seemed to not care
Outdated old food on shelves everywhere Funky, musty smell and sometimes a lusty stare

I was confused because now he is giving me

salutations of peace as
if I was a new niece

Even over the smell of pork rinds and old
chicken grease?

Finally, now things seemed
clear after all these years
truth appeared

I gave salaams back and asked why they sold
pork

and u don't put it on your fork

Don't you want for your brother what you want
for you?

Do you fear your Lord or care about what u do?
Karma is waiting for you!

He looked at me with a strange stare
almost frightened with a dark glare

He said, "well I have to make a living,

I try to spend regular charity with
giving, to my people each Friday at
Jumah."

I said, "you must serve the people where you
are,

We not your sisters and brothers like Hasan
and Jafar?"

And you say your name is Mo

Why you wanna hide the noble Mohammed?
I'm giving it *my everything* to get the name my ancestors *bled for*
Who were put outta some of their homes and *fled for*

I see you with our women in the hood and drinking at the local bar

on the side of the building with my sisters in the back seat of the car

Then you go home and give money to your kin Yet pretend to be our friend

this all must come to an end

Truth is rising up from roots and it's time to transcend

As I left the store never to return there again brain was drained and I couldn't comprehend

I wanted to be close to the ways of my original kin

One with the One and loving doing right by all

Yes, Yes Babylon must fall!

Nation of Islam

Started going to the Saturday classes
No more cartoons with milk glasses
I was ready to graduate to an MGT.

Training for war on all realms with Digni-ty
The cream of the planet and Human Socie-ty

I wanted, Equality, Justice, and I wanted to be free

Knowledge of self, self- love and every opportunity

Wrote my letter and I was in
First try; so focused, yes, let the drilling begin

Hut one, hut two, hut three
Drilling in my mind my divine reality
Mastery of self is where I was striving to be
Take these shackles off my mind and let *ME be*

First thing is first I had to get my Number 19
The garment of sisterhood designed for a Queen

Blue, Brown, Beige and White, I felt so Supreme

The wisdom with every cut and stitch Mother Tynetta crafted
Fit for an original woman not grafted

I loved learning about the beauty of my skin
My inner Goddess and the beauty within
Proper manners at home and abroad

Preparing me for my divine husband and giving
birth to a god

I was ready to be a part of a new
world Protecting our little boys and
girls

Where I'm respected and directed to be a
master

This was preparation for the real hereafter
Transforming my mind, body and spirit
Fasting, eating once a day so when God spoke
I'd hear it

Bringing out new mind, new human
kind

Waking up the deaf, dumb and blind

Net rose from my eyes and lust out of my
ear; Only Allah should I fear

Introduced back to the natural living coded in
my DNA

Classes and training weekly so evolution would
stay

When I first witnessed Sis Ava I was on high
Never heard such a sister speak like her soul
was on fire
Aligned intellectually and with Allah's desires
Oh Allah let your desires be my desires

Like the prodigal son this daughter was
welcomed back in

Was so open to allow healing to begin
I was ready to ascend

So proud to be an MGT;
Back to my true originality

EXCELLENCE THRIVING

Dedicated to Imam Warith Deen Mohammed (I was a student in his Comparative Religions and Arabic Class)

Excellence is the first word when I remember the legacy
It propels me forward in every aspect of my life
Every Sunday in class my soul shivered with his presence
Humble yet his aura towered over the universe as he entered the room
Causal sometimes even wore a Sox baseball hat for Chi, (Chicago)
Love for us to reach to that Divine personal connection was so profound

You felt it in his breathing in between each phrase/each word/each recitation
Patiently teaching, serving being the example of what we knew to be possible
Sometimes tears streamed my face as the love from his heart pierced mine
I knew at each moment each week, I was in the presence of a *TRUE* one

I would literally hold my breath and delay going to the rest room in class
Well, I call it more of a healing session

and each moment each second seemed like eternity
I never wanted it to end
His heart was kissed by the sun, so vibrant, giving, radiate and free
Reminding us that *we are excellent* and every attribute of magnificence
Interweaving, interconnecting lessons from old

That old time religion, good morals, values and striving
The Bible/Quran/symbolism/the language/linguistics/the good life Untouched by none
Each pronunciation in divine accordance with heavenly breathes
The meaning was so beyond the mediocre books in existence in society
The wisdom flowed from inner connected divinity
and he led us to that in us
Such pure life, such pure love

Every Sunday I was captured by the true love of Allah to be chosen to sit among the few in this day and this time
You thought it would last forever
but somehow deep in the core of your center you knew it one day would end
And in the divine order Allah blessed me to receive
Now will my actions replicate the gift I was gifted

The eternal love and wisdom live on

Through those who really listened and heard with their heart

When My Drop Becomes the Ocean

As I sit upon the shore looking way off into the ocean it seems so far away

I'm still a drop my ego got me caught on the earthly stay

It got me thinking I'm something I'm not

Got me thinking about nonsense and my heart sits and rots

My ego tells me I'm the queen and king and I wear the crown

But my soul crying, "no, you're just a drop" and then my heart frowns

Inside, my ego tells me "you're the greatest" that's all it sings

Just arrogant, cocky listening to no good advice, it's doing its own thing

Don't want wisdom God brings
I'm tripping, my ego was sending

me slowly off the right course so my life seems to be ending

I was getting beat down because I was just stubborn and refused to submit

Until I couldn't take it anymore!
Pressed forehead on the floor

was tired of Shaitans blows and hits
and I was tired of being hit

My heart was veiled

in jail, no one in sight with bail
because I gave in to my own low desires,
My soul couldn't take it anymore; it wanted to go higher

I gotta get *it* in this life my soul would tell me
But I didn't listen
I was covered you see

You gotta be hungry to reach your soul
you gotta literally taste it
It gotta be edible
You gotta reach to function from the universal soul powers that's incredible
because you are incredible

Finally, I dug deep to connect to my soul
and started to run and break loose
feet dry in the sand
I was still a drop about to get evaporated on land
My heart was pounding!
I was leaving the pull of my ego leaving it dumbfounded
My soul was cheering, yes this is astounding!
I could feel the breeze get closer upon my face
My ego was still trying to win the race

I did a divine Olympic sprint
Allah lifts me up and divine protection was sent

And with the biggest dive
Finally, I was then truly alive!

At last,
My drop became the ocean.

Function From the Soul
(for the pioneers)

They function from the soul
They knew Allah was in control
They function from the soul

Beaming brightness that lights and gleams
When day seemed dark their glow reigned supreme
Through dark filled paths, paved righteous dreams
into fruits so ripe, the nourishment creams
Unveiling and uncovering jewels that still beam

These are the pioneers, the ancestors with that righteous breathing
I see through their pain and hear their chants of believing
Their memories carry nations and wealth on their shoulders
Burdens sometimes were heavy as 10 ton boulders
And when some of us still slack and are ungrateful, you wonder why their spirits scold us

Sometimes intentions are not just good enough when the action undone continues to waver in your heart

You have to do more than just play the part
Must have courage like a lions' heart

Internal burning cries screamed out loud
manifested in their honorable actions women and men,
Faith filled deen connected them as kin

Their journey has been long

but mighty men and warrior women
held strong

Warrior's wisdom washed weak ones as they
held patient to allow a nation to form

When I look at their faces I see remnants of
hope
They knew how to cope
Some were even raped in chains, and hung
by rope

I feel the connection, that's why I only know
how to be real

I don't know how the fake ones' feel

I don't know how to be quiet when my soul tells
me not to sit still

From Nat Turner, Marcus Garvey, to Emmit
Till

Ayesha, Khadijah, Elijah Muhammad,
Prophet Mohammed and there are more still.

Never in denial, bringing light with the
Quran to the west, and breaking and
decoding the Bible
They knew about survival, and many unnamed,
unknown but held to truth without denial

And the list goes on and I could continue until
the earth rent asunder and sat still.

*So this is for those warriors who still keep it
real!*

Their actions are bold,
They paved the right road,
They function from the soul

He Lives for Justice

(for Imam Al-Hajj Talib Abdur-Rashid)
aka the Hip-Hop Imam

He walks with a Universal Black man stride
as if he hears rhythms in is heart

A global glide you will see no matter where
you are

Africa, Chicago, London, New York City,

Legacy of el Hajj Malik el
Shabazz His very speech roars
justice

teaching young artist about spiritual heights
and the power of voice and culture

Feet in motion on concrete
Actions activated for the people

HIV, Hunger, Right to Speak is just the
beginning of an explanation

of his passions for which he fights for
Not just on the minbar but taking it to
the streets

Allah is with him so he can take the heat
Documenting history and reclaiming legacy
Works featured globally, yet humble because
he is working for God.

Assault On the Senses

Feeling/smell/taste and touch and sound
Feeling/smell/taste and touch and sound
Feeling/smell/taste and touch and sound

We not from this world we just touching down
I grab my words from my soul and I write it down

We not from this world we just touching down
We not from this world we just touching down
We not from this world we just touching down

This assault on our senses has made us senseless

We broke and got major ghetto expenses
and we up in the hood defenseless

And when truth and liberation comes to us
some of us just put up our defenses

I wonder where these inherited habits first came from

Where the vibration of my name's from
What ancestors my uncle got his game from
Cause he still got tendencies of Hennessy

so I gotta take yall way back to the beginning
like Al-Fatiha and Genesis

Cause I know we just don't inherit bliss

But I wonder why some not on the path to righteousness

What differs those who strive on God's path
from those who fall in God's wrath
Who don't even know they need a spiritual bath

We don't function from whole souls we
function from half
Worshipping money, sex and
fame
feeding off of worldly acclaims

These so called revolutionaries, man they
losing their game,
publically displaying their shame,
like some animals that need to be tamed

This world is a devastation an atrocity
yet we got world leaders preaching
democracy living a life of hypocrisy
Got world leaders by bureaucracy

*This assault on our senses, has made
us senseless*
*We broke and got major ghetto expenses
and we up in the hood defenseless*

I say let's take it back to the old school
let's first clean up the hood and roll up on these
fools
Let's use some real 1960's gangsta tactics
and tools
Cause we up in the hood with so many
hidden jewels

that are left dormant within
It's time to fight these jinn
and diminish these sins
We got prescribed identity appealing through our senses
through false body images and botox fixes, liposuction, titty reductions and lip injections
While we up in the hood passing around STD and HIV infections
You wouldn't even know we were created in 7 heavenly stages
Cause we've drifted way back, way back to the dark ages
souls excepting minimum wages
cause we too impatient to reach our heavenly stations

We gotta be like Prophet Joseph who only had faith and vision
He was patient even while in prison

So we'll go from being programmed pimps and hoes
To selling rocks and blows
to CEO's and wrong we'll oppose

We're injected, infected and neglected, misguided, divided and disconnected

Feeling/smell/taste and touch and sound
Feeling/smell/taste and touch and sound
Feeling/smell/taste and touch and sound

We not from this world we just touching down
I grab my words from my soul and I write it down
We not from this world we just touching down
We not from this world we just touching down
We not from this world we just touching down

And only a few manipulate the minds of the masses

cause we battle everyday just to maintain commonsense and 5 senses

It don't make no sense, this assault on our senses has made us senseless

Has made us senseless

Taking It to the Streets

(for IMAN's International festival 2005)

We taking it to the streets
I know yall feeling the
heat
embracing the peace
cause you up on your feet
We got Lupe, Cap D and Manowax on the beats
So don't slumber or sleep

Allah be opening doors
from Marquette to south shore
Third eyes' open like pores
No liquor or drugs, we healing spiritual
sores
Tongues sharp like a sword
We in tune one accord
Don't sleep you can't afford
Get your shield and your sword

Artist and lyricists on a mission
with divine permission
Our souls in total submission
We're new school with a little old school
addition

Packing with truth
Teaching the youth

Healing torn souls like abesol on a tooth
Breaking, graffiti with deejays in the booth
Spiritually high like we up on the roof
We ain't faking the truth
I know yall feeling the truth
feel like Common on corners and Mos Def in the booth
Taking it to the streets for the old and the youth

Music is divine
Voices one of a kind
Let me elevate your mind
This is a divine design
I'm just so refined.

My vocals get behind your subconscious mind
Giving you that peace of mind
that crease between the time
Be *your* connect to the
divine

When the sound is so refined
Voice is one of a kind

Let me elevate your mind!
Let me elevate your mind!
Let me elevate your mind!

I'm taking it to the streets

Come on, you know yall feeling the heat
Get up on your feet
We got Lupe, Cap D, and Manowax on the beats

We taking it to the streets!

Calm Spirit

(song lyrics)

After all this time
I'm still searching for me to align
to the divine in me
so I can spiritually see
and totally be free
To be.

My journey has been blessed
forever on my quest
for inner peace, divine actions to increase
to manifest and let Allah possess
and let go of the illusional stress.

When you see the divine within
you can see it in all others then
and you can feel good in your skin
When you totally let Allah in

I ran from self
covering with someone else
trying to fulfill my void
Pretending to be overjoyed
Until I went in my inner cave
I broke down and I was raised from the grave
No longer a mental or spiritual slave
Realized Allah gave me the power to save.

When you see the divine within
you can see it in all others then
and you can feel good in your skin
When you totally let Allah in

Your heart will be bound by love

building a foundation only a soul can speak of
The kind of bliss that some can't even dream of
Tapping into the secrets of the soul
that will be secret no more

Springs of knowledge and wisdom emerge
because the illusional self has purged

When you see the divine within
you can see it in all others then

When you know yourself you know your Lord,
Then mind, heart, soul is one accord.

Divine Love

As teenagers' even adults any man spitting the right words, like I love you

Oh! sistas we give it all up, oh! we're done, oh! we're through

But what we don't realize

we're looking for Divine Love that can only come from the Creator

He created all creation with love so who's love could be greater

Aren't you tired of all the empty relationships, Oh I love you baby, Oh, I love you too

Real love comes for the Divine source, real love is Divine love given to you

(*Hook*)
Divine Love is the essence Divine Love I need them Blessings,

Divine Love is the essence Divine Love I need them blessings

That caresses your soul and connects you to your real being

this is not me or you that you are physically seeing

Our body is not us and we're not our bodies

We spend so much time on this

Are my clothes tight, my hair just right?

Of course, take the best care of your physical body, but what about also taking care of your soul
What about connecting to your real essence, what about letting your real self unfold?

Sistas some of us actually compete on who has less clothes on or who gets the most whistles and stares and who wears the best clothes Gucci, Burberry or who has the prettiest hair

You looking for love in all the wrong places

Don't you know God wants your love girl He's the Creator of all these Faces

And what some of yall got three or four baby daddy's and you pregnant again,

You got your children all confused when this madness gone end,

I said this body is not us and we're not our bodies.

(Hook)

Divine Love is the essence; Divine Love I need them Blessings,

Divine Love is the essence; Divine Love I need them blessings

We confused about this, that's why we don't nurture our soul, that's why we go through the same ol' drama that's why we never grow
But when we truly ask for that divine love that encompasses all
then you're able to love yourself, help others then stand tall

And some of yall are liars because you say you love God and everybody else too
but how you gone have love for someone else if you ain't got love for you

We so desperate, we just want to feel love from anyone who seems like he cares for us
but it wasn't real in the first place then you left looking sick with disgust
I know sistas you just want somebody to love you and not have to put up a front or a show
but God created you with love sistas, don't you know?
It's okay to be by yourself and with your Creator for a while
it's okay to take some time to love yourself, it's okay to take some time to reconcile

God says why you spend so much time trying to please them and not Me
Who's the one that determines your decree
When He gives you that divine love that's love that you can give back from your heart unconditionally

That's when divine oceans, blessings,
wisdom takes over and possesses you from
Thee

(Hook)
*Divine Love is the essence; Divine Love I
need them Blessings,*

*Divine Love is the essence; Divine Love I need
them Blessings*

So don't just try to get someone to help you in
material gain

because in the end you've only cheated
your soul again

And when the soul is activated it can
be dynamic on this physical plane

And then you two can draw from the heavens
to maintain

Because when God loves you, When God really
loves you!

And that's all that needs to be said

He'll give you all things, material, physical,
spiritual

in all ways you'll be feed

And then you'll have real beauty, not just
this thick layer of skin

Real beauty, divine beauty that emanates from
the soul within

And your false sense of self will start to disappear
and you for real will come clear

You can't measure the soul, it has an unlimited connection
that'll give you unlimited direction

This is only one ray of our physical form so
don't let your mind trick you to conform

You're a paradise being
so take your place on your throne;
you paradise queen!

You and Allah's relationship should be tight it twist
so no man or women can come between it

And when you finally get that soul mate that you've been waiting for
You're not starving for someone to tell you how special you are to feel complete once more

Your relationship will be based on divine love, power and trust
It won't be based on drama, confusion, madness and lust.

Then you're able to be that real role model for your children to imitate the crown of creation they can emulate

It doesn't matter what you've been through
we all have a divine destiny
Pray to Allah,
Please bring out the best in me!

And then you are able to have divine love for someone else
because you'll have divine love for yourself.

Divine Love is the essence; Divine Love I need them blessings
That spiritual caressing, I'm tired of stressing, I learned my lessons

Divine Love I need some seconds
Divine Love, Divine Love
Divine Love, Divine Love.

God is One

(from my play "We Are One")

Mind blocks and locks your souls in a box
Too closed, hard as rocks when God knocks

Some resist and rumble over theories
and philosophies
disagree over numbers 1 and 3
Mind seeped in debris, yet claiming to profess Thee!

Our souls are a place where the Creator resides
So we connect on a spiritual plane to the Most High
We don't wonder why, some question and deny

His many paths to reach to the Divine
to serve the Sublime
He designs and assigns to true servants refined.

They've delved deep inside
and they see with God's eyes
without greed, envy and
pride

We recite and memorize Holy chapter
after chapter

In hopes to reach what is already here
hereafter Then after we hear them we fight
over books,

Backbiting and jabbing giving each other left
hooks

So it is time for divine love to gush down
and perfume us
Let endless blessings consume us

It's absurd we supposed to serve
from many streams spring like spirits

Some locked in boxes
anyone don't look like them they knock it
Tired of hypocritical claiming to perform
miracles, to being spiritual

We connect on unseen infinite energies, it's one
God, one force, one spirit, one cause
We get stuck on labels
fables that keep us
unstable
Quarreling like Cain and Abel

We're Spiritual twins
same soul from
within
Never let titles of religion pin us in
must begin to stop allowing Shatain to win

We cry together, laugh together, praise
the Most High together

Though we walk different
paths our destiny is the same

Though we walk different
paths our message is the same
The goal is to our Lord, not about east or the
west
but the heart in our breast, the soul in our chest

Because *God is One* and so are we
from many faiths and ancestries

We chant and sing in different tongues
Praise the Most High
because **GOD IS ONE!**

A Brighter Day
(Lyrics)

*I was slowly slipping
away
and I knew I couldn't stay
living in yesterday*

*I was slowly, slowly, slowly, slipping away
Drowning in my pain, drowning in my pain
Till I woke up*

Oh, I woke up to a brighter day, a brighter day, a brighter day.

Waiting; wanting; yearning for that pure true love that enfolds inside my soul that makes you one,
man, I thought I was done

The journey has been so long
Past relationships have been so wrong but with faith I stayed so strong

Ever unfolding, uncovering, rediscovering
years of pain wrapped around my insecurities
Couldn't always see so clearly into eternity
or exactly where the blessings be.

Never thought I'd have marriage end in divorce

This wasn't supposed to be my course
In divorce court, begging for child support

Bruising my spirit, but I knew Allah would hear it.
So I broke down to pray
Stayed strong so my morals wouldn't sway
Cause I was slowly slipping away

Then one day
sensations of a whole soul came into view
when I laid eyes on you
You didn't care what I'd been through
You said it was divine what was sent to

With your soul you give life to mine
Our true realities intermingle and intertwine,
Every fiber of your being represents a real man
being true to you is on demand
You got love for righteousness, justice, truth and saving souls
Our two energies connect to make us whole

Your actions stem from our ancestors' prayers
from Africa to A-T-L

We spiritually connected, it's so fluid freely flowing
Together forever growing, you forever teaching and showing me a real man,
every hair on your body stands up in total submission,

cause you on a mission

And Allah sent me to be your companion and friend
We'll have so much success to no end
We were put through these past trials to finally together win

I woke up to a brighter day.

Tasleem's Bliss

La illaha illallah
La illaha illallah
La illaha illallah
La illaha illallah

I'm so grateful to feel that Divine unconditional love
from my Creator
The road and journey that you go through is real
but the peace inside my heart and soul validates the ills
I'm much richer from the examinations, and spiritual stimulation
He got me and I'm so close to bliss
This is a comfort you gotta feel in this life

He's so beautiful/so merciful/so gracious/so generous/so loving/so healing/so nurturing/so mighty/so perfect/so forgiving/so magnificent

He's the Greatest, to me
He's the Greatest, to me

Love Transcends Space and Time

Love Transcends All Space and Time
Love Transcends All Space and Time A
love like yours is so divine
I'm so glad that I did find
A love like yours cause you're so fine,
you're so fine

Feels like I've known you my entire lifetime cause I can talk with you from daybreak till night time

You appeared when it seemed I was running outta love lifelines

You on your deen, warrior spirit, plus you connected to your inner divine

You picked up on my thoughts before they fell to the surface

I'm thinking, can he read my mind so he could rehearse this?

The beautiful melodies of life's wisdoms that flowed from your lips

I said, "this brotha has got to be reading from a script"

But don't I have real faith and isn't this what I prayed for

Don't I have real faith and trust that Allah has more in store

Love Transcends All Space and Time
Love Transcends All Space and Time

He's my soul's reflection
We have a spiritual connection
We were the same spiritual complexion
Pure Love
We talked about building nations
and having children and owning property in several global locations
even Setting up some major corporations
but first setting a spiritual foundation We had so many similar expectations
cause relating with him was on some higher conversations
It was a quiet, deep, pure inner communication

Before love transcended
my love life had ended
Heart constantly broken and mended
My soul felt suspended
My hopes had descended
Disappointment I befriended
Brothas approaching me foul, I felt offended
Yet when love transcended
My soul ascended
Our spirits have blended
On God I depended
Got exactly what I intended
When love transcended
When love transcended

Love Transcends Space and Time
Love Transcends All Space and Time

There was no disorder
This is divine order

He talked about having sons and I talked about my beautiful daughter

Before, talking about marriage right now I use to say why bother

But he was honest, upright and wise just like my father

And conversations with him were smooth like drinking zamzam water,

He even calls me on the phone to wake me up for prayer at Fajr

Love Transcends All Space and Time
Love Transcends All Space and Time
A love like yours is so divine
I'm so glad that I did find

A love like yours cause you're so fine, you're so fine

Cause I can talk to you from daybreak till night...

till nighttime...

From the Southside of the Sun

When I was very young I just knew right was
right
Deep down in my being I knew to get liberation any
warrior had to fight till they fight
When I hear my poetry
it's like I tap into my pre-existence before my
flesh

Where the love?

I meditate on bliss
As I think of the world in global crisis
I'm filled with sorrow and pain
Yet I focus on gratefulness

Still got long ways to grow
Long way to show

In Iraq and Iran
Masking evil in Sudan
Will the world take a stand
Where the love at?

Motivation
(lyrics)

My motivation is my daughter's face
Pure soul pure amazing grace
I pray to God I keep her in a righteous place
Cause she bring me sunshine, that I can't replace
She bring me sunshine that I can't replace
That I can't replace, That I can't replace

I struggle hard to feed and clothe
Sometimes my soul bleeds and corrodes
cause I bear these weeds and loads
I pray to God I nourish her as she proceeds and grows
into a warrior on this righteous road
cause sometimes I feel like I might just fold
But then I realize that there is a brighter road
So I strive harder to reach heights that's bold
Daily struggling
and Fighting souls
Until I let Allah and let it go
and now I continue to just expand and glow

She's my motivation, my only seed
I'm planting roses and removing weeds
She depends on me when in need
That's why I got to keep it tight indeed

Some wonder why I work so hard

with no sleep and 3, fo' jobs
Feel like I'm Fighting devils with slow rods against all odds
But I'm still inspiring those near and far
Feel like a race driver without the car
Trying to teach her to be a modest queen to earn honest green
to love herself and have high self-esteem to let her spirits beam
let her taste it like she like tasting cookies and crème
But how can I teach her real family life? When she see surreal family strife
just family fights cutting my soul like a knife cause I'm a single mother but not the wife

She's my motivation, my only seed
I'm planting roses and removing weeds
She depends on me when in need, that's why I got to keep it tight indeed

I got unseen ammunition
Pure and unseen intentions
with no tension
I got Allah's intervention
to assist me on this here mission Prayer beads man I'm up all night with that inner struggle that inner fight Angels guiding me with inner light
so I'll never give up the winners fight My Faith is planted solid, stable and firm and I thank Allah for all I'm able to earn

I don't want to be a hypocrite unstable and burn
So I'm fighting for our babies till my last breath in the afterlife even past death
I don't want to be a Satan masked and possessed
I got truth engraved and blast in my chest
so I'll never take off my warrior's vest

She's my motivation, my only seed
I'm planting roses and removing weeds
She depends on me when in need, that's why I got to keep it tight indeed

My motivation is my daughter's face
Pure soul pure amazing grace
I pray to God I keep her in a righteous place cause she bring me sunshine, that I can't replace

She brings me sunshine that I can't replace
She brings me sunshine that I can't replace That I can't replace, that I can't replace

Reflection of Beauty
(for my babies Khalilah & Maryam)

When I look into your innocent face
and hold you in a warm embrace
I see your beauty that I can't trace

It comes from a place on high
It brings tears of joy so I cry

Give me the selfless love that you two
exemplify.

I clearly see and experience Allah's blessings
every day
in every way as He displays
Blessings that bloomed
when I carried you in my womb

It was really the first time I truly knew the
Creator
I mean *for Real*
I prayed continuously, endlessly
Knowing that a life was being formed
to inform the world of His greatness.

He, Almighty placed the beautiful souls inside
of me
to be a vessel, a co-creator with Thee
It's humbling with honor

That they honored me by calling me ummi and
mama
They teach me with wise words at 1 year of age

Wisdom beyond earth, giving me advice like
a sage
What a mercy and blessing
They give me love pure, true, and
unconditional when she says
I love you mommy
The most beautiful sounds

God's true servant, my babies
KHALILAH & MARYAM

Bismillah ir Rahman ir Rahim

Journal entry on my way to New York City, September 18, 2007

Allah, thank you for my life and allowing me to be a positive influence with my art. I am truly a servant and want to be the best servant. So many people inspire me and I want to be excellent in what I do being a vessel and your servant to show my love and appreciation for my life/knowledge/the path/journey/sacred gifts/blissful blessings/mercy/divine protection. I have been blessed to express and share my words that come from my soul from which you made me. Use me oh Allah to be a vessel to speak Your words and be a TRUE servant and touch the world...
Ameen

Back em' Them Days

Never weak, she speak with that ancient antique heat from the soul,
So divine reminding blind minds it's time to be whole,
See she be straight on the path so she'll never fold,
Natural food that exude from her body so she won't corrode,
Decoding codes of deception and rejection so yall might explode,
But she was foretold that she'd be bestoyed to unload these warrior odes,
Don't you know she got a spiritual glow and flow that make her lyrics superb,
Like goldenseal herbs on African fields,
She heal with them words,
From Tennessee to overseas they bumping her CD on the streets by the curbs,
Clear message with the flow so your soul not disturbed,
She be ill with them rhymes quite clever but never absurd,
And voice so fluid like a beautiful bird,
Tasleem Jamila chi town, some of the best yall den heard....
Some of the best yall den heard.

(HOOK)
I'm taking it back to them days,

When Kangoes were swayed,
Graffiti got sprayed,
Rakim got played,

Over the mainstream airwaves,
Revolutionaries were brave,
Souls were getting saved,
Taking it back to them days, them days

(RHYME)
I'm mystical like a kufi wearing sufi,

A Buddhist chanting, eating sushi,
A gangsta guerilla some say sunni,

Biblically baptized, quoting Quranic wised,
Man I own this,

Still paying Chase bank you gotta loan this,
Honing my skills so your brained strained trying to comprehend my throneness,

Queen expertise, expounding exponentially grownness,

Independent artist reincarnated revolutionary rebel but still can't clone this,

Respect claimed and demanded,

Original oracle spiritual flow and flyness man I'm branded,

Handed down landed scripts on lips like Oshun I commanded it.

(HOOK)
I'm taking it back to them days,

When Kangoes were swayed,
Graffiti got sprayed,

Rakim got played,
Over the mainstream airwaves,
Revolutionaries were brave,
Souls were getting saved,
Taking it back to them days, them days

(RHYME)
I spar my victims like a Bruce Lee movie scene, don't scream...
or don't stress
My technique will be a painless, pro-cess
I got express access, to what Mau Mau possess, blessed...
In my battle dress with finesse, mind blessed, no contest...
Produce the tracks, that compliment my lyrical freedom of press,
A MC like Guru and MC Lyte at best,

Hope you hear the codes in my rhymes real clear,
Scientifically engineered, and I'm so sincere,
I be near to the celestial sphere,
Negative atmosphere, disappear when I enter without fear,
  In submission to my Divine mission,
Uplift from the upright position, Tuned
into the God intuition,
Like a Naturopath physician, giving you that organic nutrition,
Linked to ancestral transmission,
You crave to be saved,

So I'm brave, like Harriett Tubman
freeing mental slaves,

Bringing them back home from the cradle
to the grave,

Freeing mental slaves from the cradle to
the grave,

(HOOK)
I'm taking it back to them days,

When Kangoes were
swayed, Graffiti got sprayed,
Rakim got played,

Over the mainstream airwaves,
Revolutionaries were brave,
Souls were getting saved,

Now we deep in the grave,
Some mentally enslaved,
Souls gotta get saved, Wore
cornrows and braids, High-
tops and fades,

So I'm taking it back to them days...

I'm taking it back to them days, to them days,
to them days....

What If

What if
(CHORUS)
I was contemplating and meditating in my mind
Transcending between space and time
Praying for a conscious rhyme
I feel like a woman...running outta time

What if the American Government was straight and truth wasn't twisted
If there was no war on Iraq and Iran and innocent not enlisted
If youth knew that Bush is a liar and wicked
Would the people do more than just picket?
Our life depends on this
So I'll bleed to rescue souls in need, no greed, plant new seeds, cultivate new breeds
My mission is food I eat, Dig deep in my soul and reach, put the bullets in the breech
This ain't watered down or bleached, listen to the words I speak

In the last days we living, InshaAllah, save yourself and family from the fibbing
don't let em fool you, what they do, some sins may not be forgiving

(CHORUS)
I was contemplating and meditating in my mind,
Transcending between space and time
Praying for a conscious rhyme
I feel like a woman...running outta time

America justifies the homicide and murder
They gathering you like a herder
Keep you thick with fantasy so you won't hurt her

Using trickery for teens, to join the army while they say freedom rings
get off the corner with bling
Who will pay the price to speak truth, minds afflicted?
brain restricted just like Elijah predicted
look at Katrina they wish we'd be evicted

Purify self, depend on God no one else
to feed, clothe and get your wealth
sustain your health

We should be in an uproar
So get your ammunition because we in war
but know what side you are fighting for

America not trying to educate and cultivate minds, that's why I'm blasting and bursting my rhymes

(CHORUS)

I was contemplating and meditating in my mind,

Transcending between space and time
Praying for a conscious rhyme
I feel like a woman...running outta time

*Tune in to the stratagem of war Get
the gun and the sword
Get in tune and in accord
But know what side you fighting for*

We Never Ran

Sometimes through unknown vessels
Allah speaks
Through hard times and hard rhymes truth leaks
words creep
warriors leap!

Slowly and intentionally planting words
written to invoke action and change
Spitting words into rainbows after the
rain Bringing back sanity after insane

Loving truth so we breathe in ancestral
fame Firing words of warriors into flames
Getting down in the trenches where grass is not
greener but brown from spirits that's stained

Replenishing soiled souls in the land
Some sat down but we with those who still
taking a stand
not faking the hand
We at war, so we tied our ankles like the
Sahabas
and we never ran, we never
ran, we never ran

Warriors in trenches
Heart beat is Allah and fist power clenches
Triumph in snow, sleet or rain hail that

drenches

Angels sent to assist on corners and park benches

More to the unseen than most see

Our minds not at rest until we all are free
Sweet like the nectar of the honey bee

Where children can realize and fully blossom to the highest degrees

We're focused to take their third eye off freeze

Our sleep is our meditation to reactivate our drive

Power hours charging up after midnight on high

Only takes a few possessed by the Most High
The mission is the prize

Some sat down but we with those who still taking a stand
not faking a hand
We at war
We tied our ankles like the sahabas
and *we never ran, we never ran, we never ran*

League of Assassins

All prayed, never swayed, renegade, with
my blade and grenade
Bloody like a slave trade, I ain't afraid to invade

No delay promenade like a masquerade I
won't be left lifeless, broke and unpaid

I'll distract them with a sensual smile

Then crack em on the back end coming in ninja
style

I'm piercing in quickly with the sword,
aiming straight for the target

Crew is precise; exact no room for mistakes
and margins

We blaze fire bombs over beats

Move in closer with vengeance until
they release loose biles

Cause I'm pulling wisdom even from
Akashi files

Eternal Soul
(for Namie, my angel)

When it rains on Friday right after Jumah prayer
At about 2:30pm
while driving on a slippery street with cars speeding too fast for the weather

I remember

October 25, 2002.

So clear in my vision my seeing as if it just happened all over again
A piece of myself died
She was full of vibrant life and soul and spirit and smiles and encouragement
I called her my shero
my superwoman
Did it all and never complained
An example of warrior woman in the flesh
Saw her physically two days before and like any big sister she always loved and gave me words of wisdom to stay focused on my path
Still over a decade now and it still stings sometimes
Like a wound to be reopened on that day each year
Where my bandage wears away from the rain
And I bleed again

Having to revisit the moment and repair my heart

And truly deal with healing not just existing
Made me realize that just reading in the books about the afterlife was not satisfying to my soul
I had to know; to communicate with her to experience

My yearning for connection on a higher plane became my every thought

What is she doing? what is it like?
So I meditate harder
I pray more sincerely

I whisper to the angels and shout out loud to The Most High!

To know
to truly know

And then I listen and hear and see and feel
And I know

That, that day was not the end but an opening to eternity...

Came for Solace

She came to him because his name was
Muhammad, Rahim, Rasul, Sabir, Khalil,
Mustapha, Husssain
Because with names with deep meaning that
rolled off your spirit and vibrated high

She thought she could find solace, sanity,
sanctuary
Healing
With his dhikr beads always in view, kufi, fez,
Salaams with a warm smile too
Didn't every Muslim brother want a queen, a
wife to help blossom and grow

When meeting him she was so open like
hookers legs
like Americas scandals
She trusted him because he talked of Allah and
Quran and Jennah and marriage
So she felt like heaven on a dark day
Like a sunny day by water
free to flow and let be

She revealed her history, her pain of the
molestation
the incest, the abuse by so many men
and how she continued to abuse herself by
being a dancer
woman of fantasy because that is all she

thought she was worth

But her heart openly wanted a new direction a life to be a Muslim wife with beautiful babies with Arabic names and husband with souls matching and just the same

But to her surprise he only wanted to know how many tricks she could do for him

never even acknowledged her pain, wounds but waiting to rip another part of her sores wide open

He was stuck on the story of her dancing; prancing as lustful images captures his mind

He talked about her showing him sexual favors before the wedding and his true thoughts were laid on the table

His name and meaning might as well wash away on shores

No longer noble!

She went to him for solace and to escape her past and move to a new future
But he still lives in his

Dark and tormented ruled by genitals waiting for his freedom masked by Muhammad, Rahim, Hussain, Rasul
Hiding in righteous armor

They come like knights in armor,
bright sparkling to save a sister

But truth be revealed, they are in pain as well
They are ruled by sex and worldly pleasures before leaving the mosque

They fight demons so dark, heart so cloudy they need a spark

Never to delve inside their past to grow through to renew

I AM WHO I SAY I AM!

Who are you to say what I am?
If I say I'm spiritual
Or Muslim, Islamic?

I may not read the book the same way you do
Or the angels may send me a different experience to broadcast to the universe in my poetry, music, voice or life

Who are you to say I am not real if I claim 5% or NOI (Nation of Islam)?!?!

Is my modesty on the market to be bought by you?

Are you the Creator because I know there is not two?

Shouldn't your focus be on good and correcting you

Be busy fighting inside self that I look like a blur

Yet your every existence and breath is to badger me first

Like I'm the curse

So much energy on me shouldn't Allah be your first

Your spiritual thirst?

I've tread waters shallow and deep

Wrestled with my ego and climbed mountains so steep

Allah uses me as a vessel and plants me in the streets
Wisdom beyond closed hearts embedded in me Route and journey is extremely unique
That's why I relate to all and they're flocking to me
Allah's in my heart and possesses my feet

Leading me on paths to do non-traditional works
Where spirits are broken and predators lurk
Where food is scarce and thoughts of survival is first
Where future projections need action and miracles emerge

Don't judge if my works show footprints and remedies for healing
A different approach with no roof or no ceiling Sometimes just a guided spirit
In synch with my feelings

Allah inspires as He pleases
Sees fit as He sees fit to slip through cracks and creases
With no scholarly accolades just intuition that reaches

So think before you speak and openly slander
That your faith and deeds stay focused from wander
I am who I say I am!

NAQSHBANDI WAY

Early mornings Fajr prayer 1 hour at least
On Fenton land where grass was dewy and
sandals sank in

Lamb sacrificed and children laughed in
French, German, English and Arabic and
all were the same beautiful chuckle

Where Sheikh would ask, Are you happy?"
When your spirit seemed glum

To make you remember simple things are
heavy That no matter how many deep spiritual
experiences and ascend ions, the basis of ALL
is joy, happiness and inner peace

Twirling like planets inside

Hearts dancing and glowing from tranquil
existence

Vibrations high on dhikr ALLAH!

Mid-afternoon associations we'd gather

Meded heart connected and stamped
with Divine Love

Seemed like time stopped even though we'd sit
and listen frozen for hours

Each word reached to you so personal for
your very soul

Hijabs of every form, color and style
Heavenly view with children whirling
from ecstasy of bliss energy

They are surely pure and saw the
angels dancing, prostrating and singing

Recitations were regal
Royalty turbans 7 yards wound around
crowns, Red, Green, Purple, White, Blue
Echoes of Takbirs, Allah-u-Akbar and HAQQ!

Dhikr time was near
Even though most hearts remembered nonstop
A continuous flow of reverence
Sitting in frequency electric circular space
Anything in the center would surely explode
from extreme bliss
Tears streaming down cheeks when the
angels kissed our hearts
We remembered our souls gathering in
pre-eternity
Together in perfection, harmonious freedom

Ya Allah! What a way trail blazed by those
determined
The secret behind the secrets revealed
Chills up spins chakras activated
Supreme healing would take place
Every time

The Way is the only way if you but understood!
Meaning so simple it may go over your head
I see this structure and path in all.

FROM THE COSMOS

"Dive deep into your eternal soul"
Baba Obi

Everflowing

Created by the One

gave you strong will

gem polished and you sparkle

some try and kill

I search from within up

high I ascend like

breathing

it's easy I inhale and get strength from the wind like

breathing I inhale and exhale again

Music is Life

I was born singing I
breathe music
I hear music when I wake
so loud like a Tsunami quake
soft with gentle A tones
in my sleep
It takes me to dimensions
found
That's why I keep music around

Surround sound from my soul, I sing
Triangle rings, guitar strums
as my spirit hums
Beat drums, as I dance and run
Heat comes and I stir up and wake up numbs

I was born singing I
breathe music
Stevie Wonder, Billie Holiday,
Kelan Phil Cohran, Sun Ra, Earth, Wind and the Fire
Every key and note vibrates me higher
into what was before.

It is painful sometimes to push; birth our greatness
Every note I choke and become great
Every stretch OM
ouch!

Vocal chords expanding

I was born singing
and I will continue each day, each hour, each minute, each second

To be born again

Bro. Kelan Phil Cohran

A jewel and treasure
Living, walking and breathing in our
mist Yet some miss his greatness

He said sing LOUD you're an AFRICAN
Be proud to be an African
Had me feeling born
again LOVING who I am

Be proud of your big voice
because it has to be heard
Takes pain to find your original
voice but it must be heard!
He taught me to
tap into other realms (dimensions) of my
divine self
Look within at my greatness and not at any
one else
EMBRACE my southern roots and dialect
and told me the universe will respond
and respect
To search the sky to connect to our eternity
To reverence the womb that bore us and our
ancestors

That divinity lies in your original soul
to work tirelessly to unite to be whole
Be bold, to be God's true original mold
Hidden treasure in front of our face,

Walk with such dignity, such beauty, such grace

I see him clearer now Oh!
I see him clearer now
REAL CLEAR.....now
that I'm far away

Dedicate

Oh My Lord! It feels so good to write
To leak out the folding of my right to
spy on eternity
cause I've submitted to a Higher power so I'm showered with wisdom that was suspended in the cosmos
froze, waiting to disperse onto ready ripe writers
Freedom is being taken from souls caged through each stage
from page to page

I'm like a Sage, burning sage to
evoke more sage energy so it'll be
sage synergy

Privileged to have reached this place
as I take from ancestors who left their trace
I see my grandma's noble face
so I dedicate this to untapped universes that stayed in the physical body

Be free...
Be free...

For you are infinite...

THE SAINTS COME OUT AT NIGHT

The saints come out at night, the saint come out at night, the saints come out at night!

Night time is the time to let it all hang out
When all the people come out
The saints, awliya,
the sages and high priest
They all come in bright colors to the feast
of wisdom, Baraka, healing, mercy and divine love
Soaring and pouring from the heavens
so tonight I'm putting on my vibrant orange and catching some rays
I'm whirling with the dervishes doing extra salat prayers

So morning will be filled with blessings for endless days
Daytime hours will be a sequential order of miraculous happenings
Glimpses here of the hereafter Better than 1,000's of prostrations
Your real salvation
Inner reciting with complete tranquility and silence
Only violence is your soul smashing your ego, only then streams of real love flow

Rejuvenating fallen faith

Lifting

Saints come out at night! Saints come out at night!

Feast of souls
Full from an abundance of discipline
Vibrant center of light
Seeking only the essence of God
Calmed and soothed by remembering soul chants
Hu-Allah-LailahaillAllah

Believers' hearts are lit like a
firing swelling flame
full, radiate and catching every soul in circumference
Sincerity and surrender are key ingredients

More pep and punch then the hottest cayenne pepper
More healing than any ancient herbal remedy
This is as ancient and sacred as it gets
Purifying every atom and cell of your being
Prerequisite for reality seeing
for 5th eye views
Just breathe and dhikr endlessly

Allah HU!

Warrior's Cry! Warrior's Cry!

Calling all warrior women
From Chicago, Oakland, New York, London
Egypt, Ghana and Yemen
Saturn, Venus, Uranus, Neptune, Mars, Pluto
and *all* star seeds
Gathering at the many corners of the galaxies
to bring new existence of culture with
refinement and peace
Rise up Queens let our souls feast
With attributes of the Creator oozing out of our
pores
Wide fields and dimensions await to explore
Resonating in us passing on to our born and
unborn
All unrighteous energy should be warned
The Majesty of Allah is the very breathing in
our words
From dark matter new matters being formed
you haven't heard
Our thoughts wise
with new brain cells we rise

God's essence permeating our form
Unveiled beauty attracting like a magnetic
storm
Reclaiming our birthrights
Radiate original glow, got that first light

Civilized Mothers directly plugged up to The
One

Surely this way will not be undone
Creative architects ushering in a new energy
New portals open we're navigating through
Sacred womb-mans fertile minds exploding
After this world, activates our new coding
Hemispheres merging
Old way purging
Now it's time for the new uploading
Finally broke it down to decoding.

Seven

Seven meters, seven notes
connected to the heavens singing seven quotes
Seven people in one accord
as Baba Kelan strings his cords, Harp
is ringing, I hear angels singing
Chanting circles around the sun
seven orbits; human vessels in tuned to be one
Mystical number, makes mystical actions
All lined up with the law of attraction

Guitar joins in with a seven beat
I keep the rhythm with the tap of my feet
Seven heavens and seven earths
Each note felt like I was giving birth

To a new realm, sphere of vibrations
tapping into the cosmic reality
with instrumental sensation
Felt as pure as my prayers prostrations
This is my libation
Ancestors I channeled with deeper
concentration

Seven songs, seven times
Seven rhymes, seven lines
Seven heavens

divine design

Leaders of a New School

My generation will no longer believe what they say
We see truth before we even pray
lies won't be passed down from they
exposed before it comes our way We got off the plantation
setting a brave foundation

not giving in with weak temptations
Thirsty for change so I give hydration
Revelation is reality living in high rotation
Put Shatain on permanent vacation Saints full graduation

We are walking positive affirmations
Living meditation
Breathing education

Success is our birthright and destination
Love is the answer to heal our nations
Unity born from painful separations with third eye observation

Functioning off of pure inspiration
Real innovation
Seeds rooted from organic cultivation
Let me *give thanks* and pour some libation

I AM

I am a Moor
coming to restore

your birthright from all portals and shores
Feel like you got a heart transplant

when I focus my chants Blissful
blessings that grant my
entrance to all the planets

I am Pluto, Venus, Mars, Uranus, Saturn,
and firm like igneous granite

I am Buddhist: nam myoho renge kyo
My soul vibrate high so I'm not for sale

I am Sufi, dhikr Allah Hu automatic implanted
in my cell

even a blind man can read my Chi without
Braille

I am Christ baptized in herbal truth
organically medicated decoded the Bible from
the root

I am OM that's
my home
First breath

I am Muslim, Jewish, Christian, ancient
magician

I am black, red, white yellow and brown
I am chi, she, thee, we and us
I am 5 star 6 star 7 circuits and beyond

I come with the force of Ma at and Mezan

Wisdom from the Sanskrit, Scrolls,
Injeel, Torah and Quran

I am air, ether, fire, wind, heaven, and earth
Galaxies from my womb each time I give
birth I am Tarot, tiger's eye, crystals and jade

I am hijabi, afro, straight hair and braids
created from *HU-HAQQ* eternal so I'll never fade

I am a ninja, warrior queen, a champion with blades
my weaponry is unseen so entry is not conveyed

Some say wow, she dope but how?
Because

I am ancient, African, Native and Lao
I am current, the future, still relevant and now

Belle Isle Awakening

The sun swallowed my thoughts as I sat suspended in my soul

Bathing in the natural element at Belle Isle words buried inside my memories cause I was frozen in time

Rewinding to cosmic energy where bliss is not bound

Where seeds are well bloomed all around When I was before; before and now at this very moment I am aware

Seeing with future view, energies new

Words that have not yet been spoken or heard

Old position withers away as the entire brain is awakened

OM

HU

vibrations shacking

up the dormant vessel

MALNUTRITION (DRIVE TO BE ALIVE)

We were striving to thrive

Had a drive to be alive

A drive to be alive

And now at 25
a lot of my sisters got fibroids and tumors
My brothers all stressed out from the high
noise and rumors
Don't own stores just consumers
Too much high fructose may cause some
buffooning
Short lived they die sooner

Enough to make you go majnoon
Deplete your immune
Out of harmony, out of tuned
The darker side of the moon

GMO at the corner store from July all the
way back to June

So much liquor there, you would think it was a
saloon
They ask can Jesus come and please save
us from this doom?
But a Muhammad run the corner store and it's

not Elijah with a how to eat to live

So if you complain too much or take the wrong pills
he might even threaten to shoot to kill

Outdated crap with pork chops, a death trap that might break your back
Hell they might even sell you some crack

But some of them are ballers
They got 4 cars, 4 children and they say this is their calling
But they live in the suburbs with fresh dry walling

Families eating whole foods standing up straight
while some of my people still crawling

Arteries clogged, memories fogged
we are royalty that has fallen
Brain on freeze, the drain of disease
And some of us still stalling

We were striving to thrive

Had a drive to be alive

A drive to be alive

We the original alchemist with healing wrist
Mixing herbal remedies with a cure for all this

Fist strong, never a hit or miss,' owned our own the village was bliss

A lineage of legacies
we so resilient

Brain circuits burst with our brilliance

Over achievers, over abundance, over standing we worth more than zillions

Land loaded with golden minerals
with no pesticides or chemicals
Rain rituals for a fruitful feast

Cultivating crops, we knew how to make our land wealth increase

So we will no longer accept rotten produce with dirty floors

You can't mop up our dignity no more
we're Moors that's out the door

We know everything is for a divine
reason New cycle, new season

It's a quickening of the awakening of
the uncaging of the rage

and that's why I still stand with a smile on my face

And I know Allah's plans and plots is his grace

I carry the spirit of Sojourner Truth and Marcus

Garvey's breaths and scars
A warrior without the chains and the bars

I come from freedom fighters who walked from Mississippi to Canada

We've come so far

A people of soul

A people so bold

A people so whole

A people of the right

A people who will fight

Cause we can navigate you through any ghetto or land
From the ghettos of Detroit to streets in Sudan to France, Chicago to the slums of Pakistan
Cause we are survivors of whips on our backs and blood and blisters on our hands
People of the Creator, we listen to
God's command

We will fight and save our babies any way that we can
Not all of us are sleep, some giants are woke pulling and scraping our brothers and sisters off the streets as they choke

because some of them have given up all hope

The world imitates our mamas courage the lioness blueprint
The ink that the pen sent
The skywalker, light bringers, those who re-invent
The soothsayers, the devil slayers, those in constant prayer

I'm rolling my neck and popping my gum and still getting a PHD

A scholar/mother/warrior/artist/healer/lover/Entrepreneur/teacher/humanitarian
It's all in me
They say, equality for all humanity
then you should not, because I will not rest until **all are FREE!**

WE STILL SCREAMING FOR FREEDOM (DEDICATION TO MALCOLM X)

We still screaming for freedom

We still screaming for freedom

Freedom, freedom, freedom

Free like when brains stained and chained
with pollution are unchained
Allah said leave self and come to me
shed self like snakes shed skin so you may
see like you submit to a doctor's treatment so
did he

Piercing lights that still gleam
through nighttime screams
But in darkness and trials forms
warrior's dreams
into a reality with strength and courage
that seeps through the seams, unlocking
and unfolding a reality that still beams

Never weak his speak from that ancient antique
heat from the soul
So divine reminding blind minds it's time to
be whole
He was straight on the path so he'd never fold
Natural foods got off that swine so he wouldn't

corrode

Decoding codes of deception and rejection, felt like yall might just explode

But he was foretold that he be bestowed to unload these warrior odes

Don't you know he had that spiritual flow and glow that made voice superb

Like goldenseal herbs on African fields he healed with his words

From Tennessee to overseas they still reading Malcolm X on the streets by the curbs

Clear message with the flow so your soul is not disturbed

He be real for all times quite clever but never absurd

Voice so fluid like a beautiful bird Malcolm X, one of the greatest you've ever heard

His chest breaths beat freedom, because he wanted to free them, some thought they really didn't need him

Some people really didn't see him

LailahaillAllah and never looked back
Shook crack, loved black
and Shaitan attacked

Emptied his soul of self and God resided
Man or woman can't deny it

He was more than just a guide
and like a new bride with pride, Allah God illuminated him worldwide

He was martyred in Harlem, raised to ranks with much honor, fonder that the kings and the scholars
causing commotion, across oceans
They even throwing up X's in Africa and Europe submitting to Allah's sincere devotion

Then they only had a piece of the piece Path of Islam, it will never seize
Man's flesh may perish, but the revolution never ceases
Rise up like yeast, it only expands and it increases
We feast on truth, we obese in this beast armies only increased with his decease

You see man's time was written on this physical plane and no man can take what Allah has ordained
His time was written on this physical plane and no man can take what Allah has ordained

I heard freedom in his soul so I chased it, no demise can stop rise or erase it

I heard freedom in his soul, so I chased it, chased it, chased it

We still screaming for freedom, we still screaming for freedom, we still screaming for freedom, freedom, freedom, freedom

El Hajj Malik el Shabazz was like those who were bold
They drew their power from their soul

And they knew that this physical existence has many tests
as a means to connect them to their real spiritual being before their physical bodies at rest
Don't you know Allah wants you to discover your very best

And it's not just about teaching or preaching
It was about digging deep down into his soul and reaching

He was a true one, a true one for real
and his transition from this life to the next was like a natural ordeal
It was like walking from this room to the next
This thing is not complex

It's about conquering your ego in life so you will function from your soul

and you will realize your mind, body and spirit will be whole

Now that's real free, free, free, freedom

ONE WITH THE ONE
(ACTIVATE CD)

Poetically emceeing/I'm a lyrical healer
Empress emerging/magical miracle spiller

Sent here from souls of masterminds/crashing lines/intelligence be past defined/aligned/with cosmic order I transcend the time/illuminate the blind/no compromise the grind/no water down the rhyme/tapping in divine/ninja style front, side, above and behind

All angles hit you from every degree/all angles hit you from every degree

Don't ignore/I soar high on the feminine core/fly high like Moors on eastern shores/the fear and the soul just got a divorce/I'm a fusion of a fighter and pure energy force/still a lady lacing lyrics pure synergy source

Ninja Nubian Native manipulating nature/
Brilliant, brave, and bold no reason some will hate ya
They know you major/focus is laser/for some that's danger/One with Creator, One with Creator, One with Creator

I'm the One with the One and it will be me
All angles hit you from every degree

Young age I did imagine I'd be rocking the stage/Clocking this wage/venting my rage/pen to the page

More than a groupie at the back of the stage/lyrical linguistics mon' let out of the cage/Leo linking legacies the lion was slaved/ I mentally engage/so they call me a sage/not just a phase/my spirits light can't weight/Born to elevate cause the people can't wait/the masses grasping new spiritual way/Watch you fold inside the fold of my mystical sway/I'm the Madame/bless you with vodoom and Quran/whoshu/ju du and poetry slam/heru, shomu and pencak salaam/all angles 360 hit from every degree/so your old self can't do nothing but flee/

Cause I'm the one with the One so it will be me

Real Power

No soul knows their final hour or in
what land he will devour Only Allah
knows about tomorrow
The All Seeing, All Knowing, All Power

Fertile minds sprouting up warrior camps
training in the sperms and eggs
More powerful than any plans of Shatian, the
police and the Feds

Yearning

I have a yearning, a deep yearning to connect with the Divine
I felt it at a time in my physical existence and it is complete ecstasy

No judgment, pure love, untainted

Sit up all night remembering Him Prostrating
basking in His Love; Divine Love
The highest and only REAL love

Everything zikrs Allah

Why am I not?

Divine Ecstasy!

It cannot be studied or learned
explained or rehearsed

Oh Allah don't leave me with my ego for even a twinkling of an eye

Allah hears and answers prayers
If I could just get out of the way and let Allah lead
Take over and possess No
more me or my desire

just Allah

Ya Allah, Ya Allah, Ya Allah, Ya Allah

Healing Our Wounds
(for my husband Khalid el-Hakim)

Sometimes I look at the wicked world and the pain and hate it has produced

The pain I still fight and it's so apparent in our Black and Brown youth

Deep like a rotten tooth, deep in the root

But you bring artifacts and history to tell of the truth

Going deep from the beginning of pain straight from the root

You're like a farmer with a harvest of treasures and fresh fruit

You make us think of things we normally don't think of on a regular basis

The memorabilia with the mockery of our hair our skin and our beautiful Black faces

But it's been left so bold to see in trails and traces

The oppression, the struggle, the triumph of the Black race

You make us deal with self facing our history and past

Educating the masses so we may desire to search and heal at last

Forgive me my love, cause you're not the one who I should scold and blast

You're a victim yourself who has healed from

the past

I thank the Lord for you and you bring blessings to all

May He take you to the ends of the earth with your museum as modern Babylon continues to fall

But, rising up is the righteous who have purified their hearts, minds, bodies and souls

I pray we are among them with our children great-great grandchildren growing wise upright and gracefully old

"Pure Soul"
(Khalid)

To my beautiful husband whose heart and soul I see

It beats loud chants of divine love and selflessness

Humble on the outside, warrior within
Working without complaint or tire
Allah surely has possessed you

Your quiet nature speaks so loud

It screams divine love, commitment, strength and leadership

I hear you as loud as a lion's roar

I see you even though they may not

In your city and all around the nation you will shine

With the light illuminated from the divine
So beautiful a creation Allah has refined

I am happy inside with thoughts of your pure face

Pure smile, pure actions, pure intentions

You are so amazing
I sit hours gazing
I thank Allah for you all day I'm praising
I see you even though they may not

I want to love you with pure intentions; be so open
Not frozen on my ego
No fears just unconditional divine love
That is my essence from Allah
To expect nothing in return
To love for the sake of just wanting to recognize your beauty
And acknowledge and bow to your soul
for it is pure and I see it

I pray that I may be one with you and we are one with THE ONE
So courageous together, conquering all that is not of good
Elevating our spirits so that we may be used

I see you even though they may not
and my heart and soul you got

90's on the Scene

Burst out early 90's on the scene
Message was clean gangs in chi mean
repping my dean with the fashions I'd bring
wrote hooks for friends that could sing

Fatir Fashions was born
styled artist sharp like a thorn
business was tough like a storm

Lead me to New York City went
to Bad Boy, that's P-Diddy
to clothe artist with Fatir Fashion Chi City

Man I was so young in the game
but I knew if no man could take what Allah had ordained
I'd be back stronger again

Company went soar with my partner
separate ways we departed
My soul knew one day I'd go farther
So no sadness, naw why bother
my faith was in order
Allah is the Restorer

So I dove deep in myself
Fought ego to death
sometimes it'd win
but I started over again

Daily battle to keep from sin until I
made it my spiritual friend

Married; had a baby girl
Center of my world

Love life in this community,
We raising babies and nurturing unity

Flying high on chasing our visions Future lite
with God conscious decisions

So I learn from the past
Moving upward with wisdom and class

The 90's was just the start of this legacy that
will last

Peace and Reason

Seasons for pieces of peace shall evolve,
Soul verses my ego and I wish every time it'd win
triumph over the low life, the slow life want flow life
like mercy oceans of never ending
growth where I became one with the One
immersed so I disappear into the One
Light up like Sun at high noon
so not to fry soon
not souls doom
Cry when I whiter and wander back
to temptation
Cause I've tasted purification
7 levels of meditation
medicating me holistically as I realize I'm whole
Oh Allah let my soul be back bold
mold me to that which I knew before knowing
existed before existence, before ego's resistance
So I'm persistent on the path back to the
Source as I divorce me and become He/She
Thee

As we grow
we flow
We are the saints, martyrs and awliyas
Friends who've ascended
See Allah's splendid
Battling the low life

Hold On

How can I be at such ease when she is in so much pain
like terror crying when it rains
like mountains crumpling in soft terrain
like storm wind blowing sugar cane

I send my soul to you

take hold

Love Catch Me

I exhaled my soul into the atmosphere hoping love
    would catch it
        I finally let go of my ego
        of my false self-projected

Let go of the 1st physical seen eye and opened up
    to the only reality
Forced by sorrow and sadness to surrender in
    prayer with my steps to be
        back to innocence of purity of
        selflessness

Balance

My every word is a prayer
My every breath is a prayer

I'm soft and militant

Strong and a little innocent

No halo
Combustion

Standing top on standards
Vocal swords
Vocal chords

So I conquer the interior that reflects
on exterior

Me

Bred in Chi so I know the blues
young and shy
always asked
why
Very inquisitive
God had exquisite plans
with His divine hand
Church bred
Spirit fed
5 percent
led
NOI read
learned to do for self and believe in truth
I feel deep like a root
Chant like a suf
sunni too
Hip hop influenced
soul bleeds the
blues
Bobby Blue Bland rhythm
from my heart is how I hit 'em
with that hip hop soul jazz
blues spirit soul rhythm

Rhythm
Rhythm

I hit 'em straight in the heart cause I aim to heal
much pain cured in me so my gain is real
Oh, God this is my appeal
Truth will prevail

Yes, truth WILL prevail.

Infinite Elevations
Journaling July 17, 2011 at the beach

Infinite elevations tapping into circuits of my soul

The ancestors carry

and thank them as I rise to cosmic remarry uniting with the twin supreme

Never know it all, but all is still within

Sit still as I ascend to power stations higher than angels and jinn

Been too long since female Queens been represented in full effect

respect in check and I project high vibrations of infinite waters of creation floating on

Dive in

Beyond before words and labels
I hide in dark hidden matter

As I flow from one posture to the next life is a never ending cypher

Sending ripples

On a genetic level my mission was laid
Sacred moments as you listen tuning into my
Paradigm shifting and the paths are free and clear
Spirit lead me to liberation
I realized who I am and except it
I'm a priestess, a shakyah

The universe is a university

DNA is changing and rotating coming into a new divinity
Old ancient reality

Each melody is in-tune interconnected are we
Each rhythm and sound is distinct from one
But we are in harmony with each one
We are the ONE
Only human race
Genetic trace
Creator's face

The cosmic information from the ethers transfers to our biological key to life
Unlocking and interacting Channeling and directing
Orchestrating the symphony of life

We selected to **BE**
Life beings from thee
I am life

Light
Living

We all gravitate toward the sun
sunlight, energy

I focus and observe My
destiny for the day
navigating my existence
because I carry
Immortal cells and tissues

Same origin we are all one
Now manifest in our thoughts and spirits close
to our divine
A truth revealed envisioning

The cycle

Hold your focus

Letter to My Grandma

Trying to stay strong without breaking down
I run between Chicago and Detroit like running between two mountains
Like a pilgrimage to my soul

From Mecca to Medina where its roots were so deeply planted and they sprout up in Chicago Back to the east each time I steer my wheel on I-94 going 94 miles per hour racing back to eternity

I no longer write from this realm my words are from
Naomi, Janet, Bernice, Sheryl Lynn, My mother and father's quiet strength

And Grandma Lena I called Le-my

So I write in their spirit and honor
As I held her hand she said you gonna be famous and a star
I said, "Grandma if I could just be like you, divine in this life I will shine!

4 AM- THE OPENING

4am opening
dhikr beads
and salat on knees
Take heed
power coming Goddess speed
Please don't mistake me for those with pride and greed
Well agreed
sages meeting transferring to me what u need
Magical feed
nurture you with fruit from organic seeds

Crystal quartz clear positioned on heart chakra
You may need a sedative so I won't shock ya
Coming with wisdom like ol school imams like Pasha,
Most say blah, blah, blah, blah, blah While my breathe is springing pure fatwah
Shero supersonic soul I get there before they got ya

Conscious cause you breathing now put God in it
Sparring a skillful master so I prepare to battle better
Spiraling spiritual clairvoyance so call me point setter

Look in water bowls and the future appear to me wetter
Heating hearts like sun,
if you closed you need a sweater
Suede or leather
Scroll scripted from my womb my baby scripted the letter
She came with new cosmic coded treatments, so some don't get her
But the real ones worship she; they sweat her

Walked the street with the warriors who cease fire
In the mud with youth giving 'em love showers
Late night angels force the people to flow ink power
Allah gave me shero cosmic possession so I only devour
any evil in the way of divine purpose and I never coware

Took the baton from those who came before
Vibrating higher on with the native Twais, Ethiopians ancestors and Moors
Shero thick with our royalty the Atlantic still roars
Sat under masters; saints who sent me over and forth
Mastered my chi with guru and stayed connected to source
Under pressure like a cooker heat 1000 degrees

*Please tell me if we don't unlock the
ghetto who's coming with keys*
Streets bleeding naturopathic medicine so I
don't add no cheese

Kun fiya kun are you on the side of the doom
Decreed set upon us will you feel the wrath or
bloom
Kun fiyah kun bring fire soon
Allah's wrath or blessings upon us which side
of the room
Will u hear the boom?
Where are your energies consumed?

So I'm sending your healing energy
The picture in full circuit with
beautiful imagery

Calling it a victory
Reversing broken history
Broken misery fixing open portals no longer
a hidden mystery
This is my healing, call me a doctor and
my ministry
They sent me fearlessly with sincerity
Telepathy loaded from the ancestry
Swords knowledge of chemistry
Astronomy and cosmic visionary

I vibrate on the higher plane

I tap mostly into some untapped higher
brain Free our babies' souls and minds and
let the devils loose

Ain't no more excuses, the pain, the blood,
the abuse

Armored fighting Satan's crew, its bout to be
abuse

Unlock the neckline noose

Free our babies' souls and minds and put
them back on high

Portals open now!
in the mental spirit realm,

God genes exploding remedies coded
Even though they appear worn and corroded

Time caught up with free spirits they capture
us Unseen, now seen and in god we trust

Actions thrust live
well and move
forward like U-Haul trucks

It's a war going on in the spirit and the soul

Let light workers illuminate the young and old
Whole nations going under like sinking ships
so cold

Majority rising and convening
Staying relevant is precedence

People feel, cause God's power is
evident After turbulence and decadence

Trials turn into heaven sent

Don't u know these are lyrics that the heavens sent?

Rising

Words penetrate the ghettos, mental, hearts and the streets
Concrete Babylon dissolving right under our feet
So I paint clear visions of the new horizons with my conscious beats
So little girls and boys are hopeful even though they ain't got enough to eat
They chew on parents lost guidance and they spitting it out like slimy meat
cause they blasting through with crystal energy that you can't delete

Inner-verse quiet storm, as I expel these words moonlight gleaming, tears are streaming chanting just like a humming bird
Solemnly sitting lotus flower as I bloom to be heard
Preparation style ninja training exclusive with One that's first
Mission destined spiritual weapons lyrics sharp on point
Focus keep flexible joints

This is it!
All or nothing I'm going hard
I've travelled over a decade from coast to coast
Healing on stages
Liquid love on pages

internal acclaim insight like the sages Silence the ignorance with bloodline facts

Legacy of Moors

Transforming environment and nature education all systems, medicine and high sciences

Empress rising!

They Sent ME

Sent here from souls of masterminds/
crashing lines/
Lyrical intelligence be undefined

Aligned with cosmic orders so I transcend
the time/
Illuminate the blind

Ninja style front, side, above and behind
No compromise the grind

Can't pay under the table to water down the
rhymes

Meded meded meded and chime in on
the Divine

19 circuits open/Mother has spoken/heal my
sisters with reiki and chi cause they so often
broken/choking on false perceptions and floss
and

Females on rise to bring the mezan
Liberation for we did come in the Quran
Predetermined way before we began

I rep it hard for Chicago and my sistas in
Arabian Sand
From Morocco to Sudan

From Detroit all the way to original lands
My aura been here for eons that's part of
the plan

Metamorphosed fast forwarded to develop
new seeds
Womb created crystal lightening breeds
Radio frequency tuned in and I'm too deep

Like Mount Kilimanjaro: STEEP!

Program is Maat
Cause balance I got
Left and right brain integration equals my forehead in salat
Chant (DHIKR) down inner devils
Soaring spirit level
Yesterday got shoveled
Reality hidden like mirror reflections 1,000 in view
Holographic forms all appear new Oceans of power mercy come up at shore
I heal like a Moor and they still want some more
Light of reality
Energy source not batteries
It's like I'm christening when my *Nur* is glistening
Volume high so are you listening

Other products Available from *My Soul Speaks Publishing:*

CD- "TASLEEM"- 16 Poem Songs

Featuring:
Abiodun Oyewole of The Last Poets, Amir Sulaiman,
Khari Lemuel and Reginald Robinson

DVD- "My Soul Speaks"- Live and uncut performances of Tasleem Jamila and an exclusive personal interview

To order products:
www.tasleemjamila.com or contact us at 773 599 9213.

Tasleem Jamila el-Hakim

A rare soul filled with healing power and energy, through her powerful poetry, thought provoking lyrics and unforgettable stage presence lies her true mission: to heal the universe with her various art forms, Poet, Emcee, Vocalist, Fashion Designer, Radio Host, Actor, Musician, Wife, Mother, Activist, Holistic Lifestyle Consultant and Motivational Speaker/Teacher.

Tasleem draws from her experiences growing up in Chicago, her faith, her ancestors and her numerous world travels.

Her skills evolved from youth taking dance and private piano lessons, while constantly surrounded by creativity and music. She has also studied Theatre and Fashion at Columbia College in Chicago. Her creative vision led her to fuse Hip-Hop, Jazz, Soul, Blues and Spiritual experiences which lends to her universal appeal.

In her travels, Tasleem has performed at various venues in Ghana, West Africa, New York City, Washington DC, Philadelphia, Ohio, Indiana, Chicago, Atlanta, New Jersey and many major universities and festivals across the globe.

Along with her spoken word talents, Tasleem Jamila is in demand as a motivational speaker and lecturer on topics from spirituality, holistic health to womanhood.

She has shared the stage with such artists as The Last Poets, KRS-1, Vieux Farka Toure, Brother Ali, Tinariwen (Mali), Tiraline (Morocco), Ali Shaheed Muhammad, Lupe Fiasco, Rock Steady Crew, Kindred and the Family Soul, Jurassic 5 among others.

As an activist poet Tasleem has written and performed special poetry for The Cancer Society of Chicago, Domestic Violence Programs, Peace in Streets Campaign and Youth Peace Summit.

Along with her training in voice, Tasleem studied in a special class entitled "Music and the Cosmos" with Master Kelan Phil Cohran and Composition with Reginald R. Robinson, Kerwin Young and Khari Lemuel.

Tasleem Jamila's talent doesn't stop at poetry, music and design; she also has her hand in acting. She has appeared in a documentary film about domestic violence which was showcased at The New York Cultural Museum. Tasleem has also appeared in the following movies: "Love Jones", "A Hip-Hop Journey with the Ancestors", (a film about Oscar Brown Jr,), and a cameo in the film "New Muslim Cool". Tasleem is also the star of a film by Lunar Butterfly Productions, "My Soul Speaks", and a film about Hip-Hop and Love of the Arts, both to be released in 2014.

When Tasleem is not performing she utilizes her experiences working with the youth conducting workshops on self-esteem, Hip-Hop and Poetry/Spoken Word. As a writer, director and choreographer for several productions her youth advocacy has allowed her to work with organizations such as Kuumba Lynx, Little Black Pearl, Family Matters, After School Matters, Cease Fire and IMAN (Inner City Muslim Action Network) where she is currently a member of their Arts Council.

For the last nine years Tasleem has been a radio host and producer, giving her the opportunity to meet and interview 100's of artists, activists, scholars and historians from across the world. Of the most notable icons she has interviewed: First Lady Michelle Obama, Imam Warith Deen Mohammed, Public Enemy, Dead Prez, KRS-1, Black Sheep and more. She has been featured in the Chicago Tribune, Muslim Journal, Chicago Daily, and on BBC, WBEZ (NPR), WHCR-90.3FM (New York), MIX FM (Saudia Arabia), WRFG-FM (Atlanta), WKKC (Chicago), ABC-Channel 7 (Chicago) and many internet and cable stations across the nation.

Tasleem Jamila released her first full length project, a DVD "My Soul Speaks" through her company, My Soul Speaks Publishing. Her debut CD entitled

"Tasleem" was released also under her company which features Abiodun of The Last Poets and composer Reginald Robinson, Amir Sulaiman and Khari Lemuel. Tasleem's debut CD fuses Hip-Hop, Jazz and Soul with a powerful lyrical flow. She has also toured extensively and made numerous appearances on other artist's albums and pages, including Kuumba Lynx "El Barrio Clocks Our Beats and Rhymes" album, Sound Mindz Music "The Attack of the Waybacks" album, Vent Movements "Let the Movement Began" album and Floyd Boykin Jr, "No More Silent Cries" anthology book. In 2009 she was asked to join a group of artist from around the world for a compilation CD dedicated to the legacy of Malcolm X "Necessary" to be released with three unpublished chapters of "The Autobiography of Malcolm X".

Currently Tasleem is an editor for the project

"Crossing Limits" which brings Muslim American and Jewish American Poets together.

She is also working on a production series entitled "ACTIVATE": which will be released as a CD, Blog

Talk Radio Show, and stage production. Tasleem is currently studying to complete her certification as a Naturopath Consultant and Physician.

Black Baptist Muslim Mystic: from the Cosmos is her first book release through My Soul Speaks Publishing.

As she grows so does her art...

www.ingramcontent.com/pod-product-compliance
Lightning Source LLC
Chambersburg PA
CBHW060520100426
42743CB00009B/1385